The
Militarization
of South African
Politics

The Militarization of South African Politics

Kenneth W. Grundy

I.B.TAURIS & Cᵒ Lᵗᵈ
Publishers
London

Published by I. B. Tauris & Co. Ltd.
3 Henrietta Street
Covent Garden
London WC2E 8PW

British Library Cataloguing in Publication Data

Grundy, Kenneth W.
The militarization of South African politics
1. South Africa—Politics and government—1948–1961   2. South Africa—
Politics and government—1961–1978   3. South Africa—Politics and
government—1978–   4. South Africa—Armed Forces—Political activity
I. Title
322′.5′0968   JQ1920.C58
ISBN 1-85043-019-5

CONTENTS

Preface   vii

CHAPTER   I. Introduction and Ideological Context   1

CHAPTER   II. The Growth of the Security Forces   19
and the Evolution of Strategic Plans

CHAPTER III. Centralization of State Power and the   34
Centrality of the Security Establishment

CHAPTER IV. The Militarization of White Society   58

CHAPTER   V. A Strategic Constellation of States   71
and Policy toward the Homelands

CHAPTER VI. Foreign Policy   88

CHAPTER VII. Conclusions   107
Glossary   114
Notes   117
Index   130

PREFACE

A scholar's life usually has some professional continuity. Each research project builds on earlier work, expanding or narrowing a previous study, and sometimes moving off in new but usually related directions. Rarely does a scholar venture into, for him, altogether new terra. It takes courage and patience to strike out de nova into unfamiliar lands. Courage and patience are not my strong suits. My own scholarly evolution has been much like the wanderings of a drunk—I may never be quite sure where the next step will be placed, but I can be sure that it will be related to the previous base.

In this professional odyssey that has just about reached mid-course, I began with west Africa, pitched up in east Africa, then central Africa, and have now planted my flag in southern and South Africa. That is the spatial dimension. Topically, my first love was ideology and problems of development. Then foreign policy, regional relations, and subsystemic analysis caught my fancy. Woven into this fabric came questions about civil unrest, violence, warfare, and military sociology. Each project ventured only slightly beyond its predecessor. Sometimes interests were combined, as in my book on *Guerrilla Struggle in Africa* and my larger study of *Confrontation and Accommodation in Southern Africa*. I would like to think that my scholarly growth was a strictly purposive evolution, that each step was coolly calculated, that I knew at every turn just where I was headed. That is self-delusion. In reality it was a sort of stochastic meander, filled with order and system, but a system that would drive those who live structured lives to dyspepsia, or worse.

So it was that I was wintering out in Cleveland in early 1982 when a letter arrived from the South African Institute of International Affairs in Johannesburg. After an exchange or two of letters and telegrams it was agreed that I was to come out to the institute for the summer months of 1982 to serve as the first Bradlow Fellow, a new fellowship designed to expand the research capacity of the institute, to promote working links with scholars around the world, and to enable scholars in the field of international relations to develop a more informed understanding of southern African questions. Initial communications discussed a research project about the Southern African Development Coordination Council (SADCC) or, alternatively, "the general area of regional security." But since I was to be the first Bradlow Fellow no one was quite sure how much could be decided in advance. We soon became bogged down in the hurried mechanics of travel and accommodation arrangements, and so decided to leave the subject matter general—regional security—and to work out the details on my arrival in May.

Once on the scene, I began to meet with a variety of people to talk about my research. Academics, journalists, government officials, and politicians agreed to discuss with me the southern African security situation. But there is an old maxim in sports that "you take what they give you." In other words, the best offense is one fashioned in response to an opponent's defense. In baseball, if they pitch you outside, you hit to the opposite field. In football, if they stack their defense to deny you the pass, you run. In basketball, if they pack the center, you shoot from the outside, and so forth. My own decision to examine the rise of the security establishment was a product of these early conversations. I began by asking about the research possibilities of studying regional security and before I knew it my conferee was talking about the State Security Council, or decision making on security issues. This was a subject that, in May 1982, excited South Africans who followed politics. Even people at high levels in government wanted to move our conversations in that direction. It was not my first choice, but rather my own response to their preferred subject. I thought of the sport metaphor, and decided to take what they were willing to give me. Members of the institute and its staff, after some selling on my part, eventually agreed with me on this project, although they could not be sure what the final product would be like.

The final product appeared in August 1983 as a monograph. Bradlow Series, Number One, it read on the cover. That was innocent enough. But it, along with two or three other scholarly works dealing with the growing role of the security establishment in government, appeared, to the government, like a concerted effort on the part of academia to discredit the Botha-Malan team. They lashed back at us at an unprecedented, for South Africa, press conference at which the head of the State Security Council, among others, denounced our work. We had touched a raw nerve.

This book is an extension and updating of that monograph. The argument developed at that time is retained and enlarged, although a bit toned down, I must admit. Much has happened since then, including the imposition of a new constitution, the Nkomati accords, the cease fire with Angola, and the widened and tragic civil unrest that has swept the country. The upshot is a book more than twice the length of the earlier work, and, I think, considerably better documented and argued. Although it is not responsible for my leanings and my findings, I owe the Institute of International Affairs a great debt for their generosity in establishing the Bradlow Fellowships, for the hospitality they provided, for the enthusiastic assistance of their staff, and for their unfailing good sense in relation to my project. Dr. Peter Vale, then the institute's Director of Research, was particularly helpful, as was Michael Spicer, Director of Programmes, who made many of the arrangements relating to my travel for research and speaking engagements. All this assistance was rendered at a time when the institute staff was going full out to make final the details of a massive conference at which it was hosting Henry Kissinger and his retinue. In retrospect I wonder how we got much accomplished at all.

Back in this country, the creation of this book took time and many turns. I'll never be able to count all those who shared ideas and data with me. But at least I must try to express my gratitude to a few, including Gwendolen M. Carter, John Holm, Herbert M. Howe, Thomas Karis, Richard Knight, James H. Mittelman, Robert I. Rotberg, John de St. Jorre, John Seiler, Roger Southall, Martin Staniland, and Richard H. Weisfelder. Thanks for your help: absolution for my errors. Sections of the manuscript, in various states, were presented to seminars and lectures, and discussants and members of the audiences came forth with suggestions and disputations. Included in this group is the School of International Administration and Affairs of the University of Pittsburgh, the Intelligence and Research Office of the Department of State, the Philosophical Club of Cleveland, and the School of Foreign Service of Georgetown University.

I thank, as well, the South Africans who helped me with my work. They are so many, and they deserve better than the violent present and the painful future that seems so likely. I am at a loss as to whether to mention them by name for fear that they may be tarred with the brush of association. Very reluctantly, I have decided not to "name names," largely because I have not secured their permission to do so. But, I would like to dedicate this book to all South Africans of good will. May God give them the patience, courage, wisdom, and love to find a way together out of their present malaise. Only then can South Africa assume its rightful place as a great and united African nation.

CHAPTER I

Introduction and Ideological Context

In June 1982 Foreign Minister R.F. "Pik" Botha turned up at a press conference in the operational area wearing the uniform of an honorary colonel in the South African Air Force. The Johannesburg *Sunday Times's* "Hogarth" playfully pondered that since "the doves of Mr. Botha's Foreign Affairs Ministry have long waged a losing battle with the military hawks over matters Namibian and other diplomatic diversions," perhaps the Foreign Minister was signalling that if you can't beat 'em, join 'em.[1] "Tantalus" of the *Sunday Express* was equally cheeky, suggesting that since Pik Botha has been good at predicting the future, his uniform must demonstrate that in his view the government sees its future in military terms.[2]

With playful sarcasm, these columnists are telling us what many others have openly expressed, that the armed forces, or more accurately the security establishment, has positioned itself at the center of power.[3] The South African Defence Force (SADF) is no longer simply an instrument for policy implementation. It is an active participant in policymaking. Not merely in military matters, but in wider security issues, both domestic and external, and even in matters concerning the homelands, or bantustans, and economic and foreign policy, those associated with a military perspective have gained the ascendant. Various components of the security establishment are prepared to provide intelligence, analysis, and policy advice to enable South Africa to counter what they perceive to be a "total onslaught." This term is presently out of favor in governmental circles; too alarmist, misunderstood, counterproductive—things the critics have been saying for some time. Yet policy still is predicated on a belief that South Africa is a besieged state, subject to a full panoply of hostile policies touching virtually every aspect of public life. Indeed, the very concepts of "total onslaught" and "total national strategy" are products of the military mind. That the agenda of government can be dictated by such a perspective itself attests to the extent of insecurity in that troubled land.

Over the past dozen years or so we have witnessed the rise of what might accurately be described as a security establishment in South Africa. Diverse public and private institutions and agencies concerned about security, strategy and defense have grown in size and importance in national life. Although they compete with one another for favor and budgetary largesse, together they constitute a concerted force proclaiming a parallel if not always identical perspective on state policy. What is more, because of the pervasive combative mentality that has come to see so many issues of public affairs as bound up in the defense of the South African regime, security institutions increasingly have demanded a greater voice and role in policy issues not normally associated with defense and security. By so doing, various segments of the defense establishment have positioned themselves to be drawn into the highest policy counsels. In short, the defense establishment has grown in power and expanded the range of its policy concerns beyond the defensive and strategic.

Some would maintain that the present spate of bilateral diplomatic agreements between South Africa and its bordering states demonstrate the inaccuracy of the above assertions. On the contrary, it is the very effectiveness and persistence of South Africa's militarist option that have driven Mozambique, Angola, and Lesotho to the negotiating table and may yet drive Zimbabwe there. These agreements, most of which cover important security concerns, are the culmination of an aggressive and pugnacious policy, not the triumph of those who advise conciliation. The advocates of force have gotten their way and now are prepared to negotiate accommodation on their own preferred terms.

Using a slightly different terminology, the South African Defence Department would agree with this appraisal. In its 1984 White Paper it claimed that the SADF's "firm actions" and the buildup of strong military forces have created a "successful strategy of deterrence" in which "it will be possible to conduct future negotiations in a calm and relaxed atmosphere, thereby gaining more time in which the negotiating process can develop. . . ."[11] The SADF's "preventative actions," in other words, contributed to "a peace initiative."[4] Disregarding the ideological component of these words, machtpolitik (*kragdadigheid*) achieved its aims.

Of course, this primacy has not always been so. When geographer Edwin Munger wrote his *Notes on the Formation of South African Foreign Policy* over twenty years ago, he was led to conclude:

> If one were to list the most important people making foreign policy the names might well run: 1. Dr. Verwoerd. 2. Dr. Verwoerd. 3. Dr. Verwoerd. 4. Foreign Minister Muller. 5. The Cabinet, and 6. Secretary G.P. Jooste, Brand Fourie, Donald Sole, and one or two other professionals.[5]

In that instance, not a single person was listed from the security forces or the civilian defense establishment. Something significant has happened in these intervening years that has enabled a changing configuration of power to be entrenched in top policy-making councils. And these changes run deeper than the fall of J. B. Vorster and the rise of P. W. Botha. It is the purpose of this study to explore these power realignments and to discuss and analyze changing diverse regional strategic perspectives of government and other agencies close to power in the light of the rise of the security establishment.

I. THE AFRIKANER POWER STRUCTURE

Politics in South Africa involves a great many people, groups, and interests. It is also subject to radically contrasting interpretations as to who holds power, how, and why. Regarding South African politics, explanation and analytical approach evoke almost as much emotion as the political process itself. At this juncture, it is not necessary to sketch the whole picture of political power and its exercise, nor to engage in important but time-consuming debates about modes of interpretation, approaches to analysis, and theoretical concepts.[6] Rather, it is necessary to sharpen our focus on power at the center, and to examine the basic marrow of Afrikaner power.

Since gaining control of government in the 1948 election, political power in white South Africa has been centered in the National Party (NP), and in various ancillary organizations that speak for the volk, the Afrikaner nation. To understand state politics all other forms of political power must be viewed insofar as they affect or are affected by the Afrikaner power structure. Thus black power, although growing in militancy and significance, is thus far constrained by the Afrikaner-cum-white power structure, and in turn contributes to a weakening or solidifying of that power. As much as it is to be criticized, it must be appreciated that Afrikaner power is the benchmark against which all other claimants to power must be measured. Their dominance of state power has not been seriously challenged for as long as Afrikaners have determined that their security and "survival" as a unique nation necessitates the unyielding and virtually unrestrained assertion of their control.

The Afrikaner nation is not monolithic; indeed, it never has been.[7] Although the insistence on Afrikaner unity has been a useful tool in muffling discontent and disagreement, the National Party has never fully achieved that end. In fact, criticism is possible, provided it is done properly—that is, according to the "rules," within the "right" channels, circumspectly in an acceptable language, and as long as it is not designed to or does not have the effect of embarrassing the leadership of the volk. The present schism in Afrikaner ranks, symbolized electorally by the

Conservative Party and the Herstigte Nasionale Party and by the challenges to P. W. Botha's leadership within the National Party, is but the latest manifestation of a nation in ferment. A *broedertwis*, a brothers' quarrel, it is called, and it runs deep through the volk.

Also reflecting that ferment is the running battle between various organizational expressions of the nation, the Party, the Afrikaner Broederbond, the Afrikaans language press, the universities, the Dutch Reformed Church, the Afrikaner business, artistic, and intellectual communities, and, equally compelling, the struggle within each of these institutions and groups for control. But significantly, through its more than thirty-six years in power, the National Party has weathered all storms and schisms, and it has managed to dampen the divisions within Afrikanerdom and to solidify its role as the principal political voice of the volk.

As a small opposition party in the 1930s, the National Party was but one of the components of the Afrikaner ethnic movement (*volksbeweging*). Through the years it has grown and consolidated its position and in the process managed to outlast parallel claimants for paramountcy. Yet within the nation and the Party, opportunities for dissent and individuality can be seized. There is a surprising measure of grassroots democracy within the nation and Party. The Party's federal structure and its constituency relations with the provincial parties have heretofore assured popular government for the Afrikaner minority. Yet, when it comes to policy making, the Party amplifies its centralist tendencies. The Federal Council prevails over provincial congresses with regularity and almost cavalier assurance that the provincial bodies will follow obediently.

Perhaps more expressive of real power in the Party are the Party caucus and the cabinet. The caucus is comprised of all NP representatives in the House of Assembly and, until its demise in 1980, the Senate. It chooses the Party leader and it helps determine NP strategy while parliament is in session. The cabinet, however, has generally been the effective policy-making body of the Party. As such the cabinet demonstrates the relatively narrow parameters of power in the country. At the Party's highest level, the cabinet is an elitist body in the midst of an ostensibly populist (albeit ethnically exclusive) movement.

Cabinet power rests on trust afforded it by caucus and on reliance upon superior information provided by top-level civil servants and bureaucrats. The composition of the cabinet, which is most significant in shaping governmental policy and the party line, is a product of prime-ministerial leadership plus the political necessity of appointing provincial leaders, themselves elected by provincial party congresses. Cabinet balance provincially, ideologically (within the party), and with the inclusion of one or two English speakers, limits the prime minister further.

Each prime minister has his own operating style, but by and large, each has had to conform to the demands of party structure and Afrikaner expectations. Within those sometimes vague and sometimes rigid parameters there is considerable play. The tenures of H. F. Verwoerd, B. J. Vorster, and P. W. Botha reflect their personalities, their perceptions of the issues and the range of politically acceptable alternatives, and the situational variables of the day. Verwoerd was an overpowering figure in the Party and once having asserted himself, was virtually authoritarian. Vorster's tenure saw a more relaxed, consensus-building approach to Party leadership as the Afrikaner business interests rose in prominence. P. W. Botha, himself a professional politician, contributed to the rise of the bureaucracy, the defense establishment, and the career politicians. Party loyalists, especially those close to P.W. Botha, have moved into positions of authority. In the process of these changes, the Party instruments have been downgraded in political significance. In the top decision-making councils, they have been superceded by governmental and, to a lesser extent, selected members of the bureaucracy.

Playing their parts in this kaleidoscopic process of power manipulation and consensus formation have been an increasingly outspoken Afrikaans press, a quiescent Dutch Reformed Church with pockets of dissent, and the Broederbond, a closed and self-perpetuating secret debating society that seeks to contain divergency among Afrikaner leaders. Its power has eroded markedly in the past decade or so.[8] In 1984 a new, more reactionary opponent of the Broederbond was formed, the Afrikanervolkswag. It bills itself as a "cultural organization" that is determined to unite conservative opposition to the government's modulated changes.

As challenges to Afrikaner power become more serious and threatening—most notably among blacks and in the regional context—practitioners of applied power, professional experts in security and coercion, have come to join traditional elements of Afrikaner power. Because of their expertise and substantive role in defense of the status quo, and because of the relatively clear consensus in the National Party on the efficacy of a coercive maintenance of order, the centrality of the security establishment is made palpably evident.

II. THE SECURITY ESTABLISHMENT

The evidence of this centrality will become obvious as I delimit and define the security establishment. In this context, the security establishment includes all those individuals and institutions, whether a formal part of the governmental and administrative apparatus of the state or attached to private and parastatal organizations, that are chiefly concerned with the maintenance of the South African state primarily by developing and employing the coercive instruments of the state or by weakening by various means the coercive arms of hostile states and movements. It is a definition that is consciously inclusive in order to discuss the full extent of security concerns.

First and most obviously the security establishment includes the South African Defence Force (SADF), the Department of Defence, and the South African Police (SAP), particularly its paramilitary units. Incorporated as well are the various branches of the intelligence community (the National Intelligence Service, the Military Intelligence Section, and the Security Branch of the Police). Some governmental parastatal corporations, particularly the industrial giant Armscor, are defense-oriented, as are dozens of private firms that do work on subcontract from Armscor. The intellectual community, including private and quasi-official think tanks, has also been recruited into this constellation of groups. The official vehicle for coordinating and expressing the views of these disparate components has been, of late, the State Security Council (SSC) and especially its secretariat.

All these groups are deeply engaged in the debate over defense and strategic policy and, moreover, have contributed to a widening delimitation of strategic affairs. Yet matters strategic have come to be seen by those in power as having an expanded, political purpose. State policy in strategic terms involves the maintenance of the regime, including its domestic features as well as its territorial integrity. In that regard, those who control the security instruments of state contribute to the determination of the internal order of things. The National Party, although it dominates government and is not faced by any serious partisan challenge, finds itself increasingly dependent on the coercive machinery of the state to maintain itself in power. At the same time, the Party as an institution seems to be becoming less relevant in policy-making terms. Less relevant, it should however be pointed out, only in relation to past South African experience. In the context of a functional yet competitive one-party state, the purpose of the ruling party falls away, and its support is in danger of atrophy. Lacking serious electoral challenge, there was little reason for the NP to maintain or update its constituent machinery. The potential appeal of the Progressive Federal Party (PFP) and the New Republic Party (NRP) has always had built-in ethnic and social bounds. It may be ironic that the Conservative Party and the HNP challenges from within Afrikanerdom may at once be the most serious electoral threat to the NP and the opposition that reinvigorates the party, in terms of policy, ideology, and organization. Although it may be premature to suggest that the state may be ready to supercede the NP as the font of ideas on how to maintain white power, there are subtle yet important changes occuring in the links between those two institutions.

III. BACKGROUND TO THE SADF IN POLITICS

The armed forces of South Africa for years displayed a multiple split personality. They were very much the product of a dual heritage. First, they were an outgrowth of the British imperial tradition of a standing professional force. Second, South Africa grafted onto the regular forces vestiges of the commando model employed earlier by the Afrikaners or Boers, especially as they defended the frontiers, organized raiding parties against the indigenous black peoples and their property, and as they resisted British expansionist efforts to seize the entire subcontinent. Of late, managerial models of armed forces in highly industrialized states, especially the United States, have helped shape the organizational character of the SADF. At least insofar as the white population is concerned, the forging of a single white South African "nation," although by no means complete, is considerably more advanced today than during the first decades of the Union of South Africa.[9]

Afrikaners have long harbored a healthy distrust of standing armies. In the Boer wars, and since independence during the 1914 Boer uprising known as "the Rebellion," when Union involvement in World War I on behalf of the British Empire prompted bitter-enders to take up arms against the Union government and its Defence Force, and when the Union Defence Force (UDF) harshly put down the 1922 miners strike on the Rand, their experiences convinced Afrikaners that standing armies were designed to repress them and not to protect them. Among Afrikaner nationalists, the UDF had long been identified with the "pro-British" elements in South African ruling circles. The long-standing distrust of General Jan Christian Smuts—whom Afrikaner nationalists called "slim Jannie," too clever or slick for their tastes—came to be reinforced repeatedly as he deployed UDF units against Afrikaners on behalf of British interests.

Once the First World War had ended, the South African authorities saw the UDF as largely a dutiful instrument of the state designed to defend the borders. Since there was at that time no serious and immediate threat to South Africa's territorial integrity, there was little point in bearing the financial burden of a ready defense force. On that, both Afrikaners and English-speakers could agree.

Virtually until the eve of South Africa's entry into World War II, the UDF had been politically quiescent and, as a result, militarily weak. At the time of South Africa's 1939 decision to ally with Great Britain, the UDF consisted of only a slim complement of Permanent Force officers and other ranks, plus around 14,600 Citizen Force men—that is, civilians who had been subject to military training and who periodically trained for deployment should they be called into active service. Equipment and supplies were inadequate, obsolete, and badly maintained. The minister of defense during the 1930s, Oswald Pirow, displayed little aptitude or interest for modernizing the UDF. South Africa was, after all, thousands of miles remote from potentially hostile forces. If the Union were to be endangered, the threat would be expected to come from Europe or European regimes in Africa. Neighboring territories posed little danger to the Union. Small wonder that the armed forces had been regarded as more important ceremonially than operationally and had been allowed to shrink.

The growth of the Defence Force in World War II was but a temporary aberration in policy. This was confirmed by the rapid demobilization after the War and a further postwar deemphasis on military preparedness. The electoral defeat of the government of General J. C. Smuts in 1948 brought to a close an era in South African politics. Although General Smuts was in many ways the embodiment of the UDF, the Defence Force had through the years played virtually no role in domestic politics. And because the UDF had been regarded as an institution very much dominated by English speakers and molded along British lines, it fared badly during the first years of National Party government.

The National Party government's initial policy agenda concentrated on the systematic construction of the apartheid state. Questions of racial separation and dominance and an elaborate legal apparatus had to be fashioned to secure what was an inherently inequitable and unpopular regime. Once having set in motion these distinctive race policies, the government turned to remaking the UDF and the SAP to eradicate the vestiges of the imperial mentality and English-speaking dominance in high ranks. All governmental institutions were converted into apartheid institutions to strengthen the party's hold on the state apparatus. In the process loyal Afrikaners were favored. Many British-trained, English-speaking officers were pushed into premature retirement. They were replaced, with intended irony, by loyal Nationalists, many of whom had no military or police experience. Indeed, some nationalists resisted or sought to sabotage the war effort or had organized against the Smuts Government during the war.

A defense amendment act required fluency in both languages for all UDF officers and NCOs and for all men seeking enlistment in the Permanent Force. Innocuous enough on the surface, this measure effectively discouraged the recruitment of English speakers, by and large less inclined then to be bilingual and obviously sensitive to a discriminatory policy if they moved up the ranks. Replacements in the officer corps were largely Afrikaners with little or no combat experience. Regiments with long and proud traditions, designations, uniforms, and insignia dating back to colonial times and invariably identified with segments of the English-speaking community, lost their historic identities. New uniforms and insignia were introduced. Afrikaners became more deeply entrenched in positions of authority throughout the defense forces, the police, and the ancillary organizations associated with security. The decision taken in the October 1960 referendum to establish a republic and its subsequent implementation on 31 May 1961, were the symbolic and sentimental capstones to this policy.

Yet large numbers of Afrikaners positively supported war mobilization at the risk of being ostracized as "traitors" to their "nation." The division of white South Africa was as much a division within Afrikanerdom as it was between Afrikaners and English speakers. The war was the emotional catalyst that brought into the open the latent social cleavages among whites that had temporarily been glossed over.

Throughout the 1950s, the defense forces were not involved deeply in policy consideration or implementation, and not at all in policymaking. Even into the 1960s, as the prospect of domestic civil unrest and external military threat on the "border" (expansively defined) grew, the defense forces sought to maintain a low profile. Nonetheless, the situational variable characterized by growing black dissatisfaction and international criticism and rejection meant that state security would have to play an ever more prominent role in governmental thought. There were guerrilla wars smouldering in Rhodesia, Mozambique, and Angola, and the SADF and SAP were surreptitiously entangled in one fashion or another in each of these conflicts. Involvement in the Namibian war was just beginning to expand as the SADF replaced the SAP as the principal line of border defense.

Despite the growing perceived need for larger and more efficient coercive arms, there was never complete agreement on how best to deal with the dual domestic and external challenges. Competition between various intelligence branches was one result. Jurisdictional disputes and institutional jockeying for position marked their relationship. Likewise, there was no clear agreement on the division of labor and the mode of deployment of the various armed forces. Considering South Africa's commitment to military defense, it is surprising how little systematic planning took place.

Other than low-level projections regarding budgeting, manpower, and weapons procurement that began in the late 1960s, it was not until 1977 that the Strategic Planning Section of the SADF was created. Despite P. W. Botha's reputation as a planner, long-range strategic thinking came late to the SADF. Nowadays, strategic planning functions take place principally in the secretariat of the State Security Council. Increasingly, however, the various security groups sought an expanded role in policy determination, first with regard to their own assigned bailiwicks, and later in related policy areas such as foreign affairs, domestic security, the economy, and eventually practically every facet of state concern. It is this pattern that is to be chronicled and analyzed in this study.

The gathering influence of the defense establishment has not gone unnoticed or unchallenged. Although considerable effort is expended to shield the process from public scrutiny, to see it as a conspiracy is incorrect. Nor can this trend be attributed to a conscious scheme on the part of individuals or institutions to seize control of government or to inflate their power in order to strengthen the security establishment or parts thereof. Much information on these changes at all levels is a matter of public record. But it is necessary, if the process is to be understood, that interested observers ferret out the information and that they engage in logical and additive analysis, even if the data lead to conclusions that make them uneasy.

IV. THE IDEOLOGICAL CONTEXT

Central to an understanding of the rise of the security establishment is an appreciation that South Africa's governmental officials live in a world that they perceive to be fundamentally hostile to South Africa, a world whose attitude can be encapsulated under the rubric "total onslaught."

It would be helpful at this point to define "total onslaught," since this term, despite its recent down play in governing circles, forms the basis for so much of South African state policy. Fundamentally, total onslaught can be viewed from at least two angles. First, there is the perceptual or subjective conception of total onslaught. This shapes the ideological and political atmosphere in which decisions are taken. Alternatively, total onslaught might be examined in objective terms. Is there a total onslaught against the Republic? Or better, to what extent do the perceptions of governmental policymakers coincide with reality with respect to total onslaught? An objective assessment of the phenomenon rather than the perception of that phenomenon would help in evaluating the extent to which policy predicated on this doctrine is likely to succeed. Not that policy based on a faulty reading of empirical reality always fails. In cases of asymmetric distributions of power and wealth, policy ill-founded may successfully blunder or muddle through, in spite of misperceptions. United States foreign policy, when it brought inordinate force to bear on problems, sometimes succeeded. So, too, did some features of British naval policy in the nineteenth century, early Hitlerian military strategy, and some aspects of Soviet domestic and foreign policy. Because they were costly "victories," one might argue that they were not successful according to cost-benefit criteria or in terms of larger social standards of success. To caricature the issue—suppose intelligence reports indicate a possible infiltration from a neighboring territory, and the government mobilizes 50 percent of the available manpower into the defense forces to the neglect of other social needs. These forces are then sent to the border, and the infiltration never occurs. Defense spokesmen after the fact may argue that this mobilization "succeeded" in deterring invasion and that the territorial integrity of the state was maintained. But at what cost, if the same end could have been accomplished with far less manpower?

South African policymakers have taken care to spell out their own views of the total onslaught. The "total onslaught," General Magnus Malan says, "is an ideologically motivated struggle and the aim is the implacable and unconditional imposition of the aggressor's will on the target state."[10] The enemy uses all means at his disposal. The onslaught is not just military: it is political, diplomatic, religious, psychological, cultural, economic, and social. General Malan again: "South Africa is today . . . involved in total war. The war is not only an area for the soldier. Everyone is involved and has a role to play."[11]

This onslaught is inspired from abroad and coordinated by the communist powers. At least for public consumption, the Soviet Union is regarded as the root cause of discontent and instability in the region. Marxist leaders are diabolically using newly independent black states and black nationalist movements for their expansionist designs. According to Government's *White Paper on Defence and Armaments Supply, 1982,*

> the ultimate aim of the Soviet Union and its allies is to overthrow the present body politic in the RSA and to replace it with a Marxist-orientated form of government to further the objectives of the USSR, therefore all possible methods and means are used to attain this objective. This includes instigating social and labour unrest, civilian resistance, terrorist attacks against the infrastructure of the RSA and the intimidation of Black leaders and members of the Security Forces. This onslaught is supported by a worldwide propaganda campaign and the involvement of various front organizations and leaders.[12]

In a censure debate in 1978, P. W. Botha as Minister of Defence told the House of Assembly:

> South Africa is experiencing unprecedented intervention on the part of the superpowers. . . . The Republic of South Africa is experiencing the full onslaught of Marxism and it must not be doubted that the Republic enjoys a high priority in the onslaught by Moscow. All the authorities on strategy agree on this point. However, South Africa is also experiencing double standards on the part of certain Western bodies in their behavior towards her.

They are doing this in an attempt to pay a ransom to the bear whose hunger must be satisfied.[13]

Since the Western world is calling for major changes in racial policies in South Africa, the West is itself viewed as part of the problem rather than part of the solution. South Africa stands virtually alone.

Within the country, opponents of the government are said to be either in league with the Soviet Union, being used by Moscow, or inadvertently assisting revolutionary forces. Insofar as opposition parties attack the government "they do not care that their complaints sometimes play into the hands of those powers that are bringing pressure to bear on South Africa."[14] Opposition parties, other domestic groups, and individuals also come under fire for facilitating the "total onslaught," among them academics, the press, and church leaders. Symptomatic is a 1983 parliamentary debate in which the minister of law and order criticized Tom Lodge of the University of the Witwatersrand for labelling African National Congress sabotage acts "armed propaganda," and for appearing to admire the ANC insurgents' "professionalism, expertise and courage." A reporter for the *Star* of Johannesburg was also scored for using the same term, "armed propaganda."[15] The minister insisted that the term "terrorism," rather than "armed propaganda," was politically less loaded. The latter term, he felt, was too apologetic. After carrying on about this term, it seems fitting that later in the session the minister of defense himself should employ it in reference to the 1982–83 sabotage.[16] Bishop Desmond Tutu, 1984 Nobel Peace Prize winner and Anglican Bishop of Johannesburg, also has been excoriated for a speech in America in which he called the SADF the "real terrorists" in Namibia. "Those people are only benefitting our enemies and they are not doing us any favours," said the minister of law and order. To the government, those who bring bad news are often treated as if they were the perpetrators of that news.

According to a 1982 public opinion poll, there is evidence that the white populace, subject to continual rhetorical assault and reinforcement, has come to internalize this generalized social anxiety. When asked if "the communist threat against the country is exaggerated by the government," 80 percent said they were either "inclined to disagree" (35.1%) or "definitely disagree" (44.8%). Even among supporters of the opposition Progressive Federal Party a majority (56.1%) perceives a serious communist threat to South Africa. Two years later this survey was replicated with practically identical results.[17] Every raid into Angola and Mozambique, every cross-border strike was used to reinforce this viewpoint as arms, literature, and captives were displayed to confirm the Soviet penetration of the region.

Virtually every facet of public life and many facets of private life, therefore, can be seen as part of the total onslaught. Since 'the onslaught directed at South Africa is considered to be communist-inspired, then South Africa must be regarded as a keystone in the defense of "the whole free Western world." The West, by refusing to appreciate the centrality of South Africa's strategic location, mineral wealth, and highly developed economy and polity, is practically collaborating in its own demise.[18] The contest is more than political; it is ideological and even religious. "It is a struggle," says the Manichean prime minister, "between the powers of chaos, Marxism and destruction on the one hand and the powers of order, Christian civilization and the upliftment of people on the other."[19]

Adhering to the idea that the Soviet Union is aiming its foreign policy principally at southern Africa and especially at the last bastion of "Christian Western civilization" there may be flattering, but it is not accurate. In a way, it is a politically functional equivalent of the Ptolemaic theory of the universe. The planets, the sun, and the stars do not revolve around the earth. Nor is South Africa central to superpower thinking. It may be comforting to the collective egos in Pretoria to know that they rule over such an important patch of earth. And it may be expedient politically to justify sacrifices and the acceptance of policies the citizenry might otherwise reject.

There is a historical parallel in the early history of the Bolshevik state. In the early 1920s, Bolshevik ideologues coined the concept of "capitalist encirclement." There was just enough truth in it to lend it credibility. The Soviet state tried to portray itself as an innocent victim of foreign intervention and antagonism.

In those days all policy was made relative to the pivotal "fact" of capitalist encirclement. Lenin had decreed that "all the events of world politics are inevitably concentrating around one central point, namely, the struggle of the world bourgeoisie against the Soviet Russian Republic." The Comintern repeated and amplified this line endlessly. All was subordinated to the contest to avoid the full blast of capitalist encirclement. Could this be Botha's "struggle between the powers of chaos . . . and the powers of order"?

There were occasional variations on the theme to play upon the divisions in the capitalist world and the need for "peaceful coexistence." Similarly, Pretoria varies its line periodically to try to take advantage of conciliatory possibilities among its neighbors. Whether it has been the "outward policy," "detente," constellations of regional states, or the current drive toward joint security treaties and nonaggression pacts, an element of policy flexibility is needed. But through it all, the threat is highlighted, and policies predicated on that threat prevail.

There had been ample evidence that the menace confronting Soviet society from beyond the borders was founded not on the actual intensity and depth of foreign hostility to communism and the Soviet Union, but on the domestic need to rationalize high levels of military preparedness, Soviet expansionism, and the continuation of economic sacrifice and political dictatorship at home. Likewise, the hostility to apartheid is genuine, and the threat is not imagined (although it is exaggerated). But it appears that such perspectives can generate a momentum hard to resist. It is tempting for Pretoria to fasten on the enmity of black states (prompted largely by South Africa's own domestic racial system and the repressive regime established to defend it) and to accentuate that enmity for other purposes. For example, this enmity has been used to discredit and isolate domestic opposition. In part it also serves to justify the militarization of segments of South African society. It has also been employed to persuade South Africa's Western associates that Pretoria, by sharing common enemies, is worth supporting.

South African hawks never tire of criticizing the West for failing to appreciate the Soviet threat. One commentator writes:

> The reasoning by Western governments that South Africa is in fact responsible for the Soviet presence in Southern Africa, is well known and displays a tragic lack of understanding of Soviet behavior. This kind of attitude has become a source of instability in Southern Africa itself.[20]

In several respects Pretoria misreads the West on this issue. Western governments, such as those of Ronald Reagan in the United States, Margaret Thatcher in Great Britain, and even the German and French governments, are very impressed by the strategic, economic, and psychological dangers posed by a communist global challenge. They are anxious about Soviet power in southern Africa. But they realize, as well, that apartheid is morally unacceptable, and that a too close identification with a racist government in Pretoria would be costly in terms of their relations with third world governments. It would, they fear, provide the Soviet Union with further avenues of access and influence. Although there is some ideological sympathy in the West with Pretoria's strategic aims, this tends to be offset by the National Party's insistence on racial separation and the destruction of civil and political liberties in South Africa.

Pretoria's dichotomous world view is by no means unique. In a grotesque way it is reminiscent of Joseph Stalin's "two-camp image" of the late 1940s and early 1950s. According to this image, a state was regarded as either prosocialist or, ipso facto, antisocialist. This view, in turn, led to its mirror image in the United States as Secretary of State John Foster Dulles took up the categorical perspective. Such a view has a further tendency to become a self-fulfilling prophecy, whereby governments that wish to remain nonaligned are ostracized. They are expected to choose sides. How, it might have been asked of them, can you remain neutral or uncommitted in such a moral contest? To be neutral and critical of both sides means that you thereby must favor the other side—at least this is what the ideological contestants are inclined to say. Neutralism can have the effect of forcing parties by default into one camp or the other. By refusing to take sides, someone decides for you.

A contemporary analogue can be found in President Ronald Reagan's view of the ideological struggle between the Western democracies and the Communist bloc, between the forces of good and the forces of evil. To an audience of evangelical Christians, the President warns of the "aggressive impulses of an evil empire." "There is sin and evil in the world and we are enjoined by Scripture and the Lord Jesus to oppose it with all our might." The Soviet leaders "preach the supremacy of the state . . . and predict its eventual domination of all peoples of the earth—they are the focus of evil in the modern world."[21] In theological terms Reagan talks of a "crusade for freedom," a holy war, a "global campaign" to destroy Marxism-Leninism and to relegate it to "the ash-heap of history."

Reagan's combative strategic mind-set seems perfectly compatible with that of the leaders of South Africa. It is intended to unify and galvanize support for anticommunist regimes currently in power. But this mind-set holds the danger of alienating the uncommitted and in the long run may well be a divisive feature of domestic politics in many countries, including the United States. Moreover, it is a prism that distorts reality rather than a lens that provides an accurate reading of world issues. Repeated expression can lead to self-deception and self-delusion—a faulty basis for making policy. Just as such a world view can be counterproductive domestically, when applied with uncompromising rigor in foreign affairs it narrows the range of policy options. In both the United States and in South Africa, policy implementation is less rigid than is rhetoric, even though the policy-making process can become contentious when issues are posed in ideological and pseudoreligious idioms.

It is not our responsibility to analyze empirically the concept of "total onslaught" and the world view that emanates therefrom. Suffice it to say that the acceptance of such a view tends to emphasize a dependence on those instruments most identified with physical resistance and coercion, notably the armed forces and their support institutions, and to a pervasive atmosphere that is suspicious of dissent and even of alternative proposals and hard-hitting criticism. In the same breath that he states that he rejects the "war mentality," the prime minister warns that

no State which confronts Marxism, no State which wishes to preserve itself in an orderly way, can dismantle or weaken its forces of law and order in this struggle, for Marxist and Russian expansionist forces believe in one thing only, and that is power, military power, military domination, military imperialism.[22]

In such an apprehensive atmosphere a confusion develops (and is consciously fostered) between white survival and the maintenance of the apartheid system (along with its creator, the National Party). To lose control is to surrender, and if apartheid means anything, it means control. That the South African state can actually be saved by restructuring the state in ways quite different from those suggested or entertained by its present leadership is to think the unthinkable. This does not mean that change is beyond the National Party regime. In fact, one vital aspect of the counterrevolutionary strategy is to maintain the initiative, to introduce proposals for modulated change, to rewrite legal instruments and reconstitute the polity, to blur the lines between formal segregation and integration, to experiment, to disarm critics by revising the trappings of apartheid without tampering with the essentials.[23] This process enables those in charge to control the pace and nature of change: or so it would seem. Whether it will unleash hostile forces moving in unexpected directions (as the right-wing Conservative Party contends) is another matter, one that is hotly debated in various forums.

There is little point in discussing the objective conditions that led to the rise of the defensive, some would say siege, mentality among those charged with state security. The isolation of South Africa and the mounting levels of violence in the region and the country have been widely recognized and analyzed.[24]

While there is a serious threat to the South African regime, one might take issue with Pretoria's current diagnosis of regional and global affairs. Undeniably, South Africa is the target of virtually universal criticism and condemnation of its domestic racial order. But criticism and condemnation hardly constitute onslaught, least of all *total* onslaught. It is stylish and politically advantageous to "attack" (an unfortunate word for verbal actions) South Africa. Moreover, there are genuine moral and philosophical misgivings about South Africa's system. The judgments of many people and governments are well founded, and they sincerely want apartheid ended. But most of them are not prepared to participate in a crusade or even in economic measures to undermine the Republic. To accuse such people and governments of joining a Marxist-dominated total onslaught is simply wrong.

In light of the above, one might also question the extent to which the onslaught is directed from Moscow. Or is it a series of ad hoc and sometimes coordinated responses to the same phenomena? Agreed, the Soviet Union would be thrilled to see political instability in southern Africa or, better in their eyes, a sympathetic socialist government in South Africa.

But for the Soviet Union it is a matter of priorities. The USSR has other, more pressing concerns in world affairs—Poland and the other East European satellites, the global nuclear balance, China, the Middle East, Afghanistan, the pathetic performance of the Soviet economy, and the struggle for succession within the Communist Party of the Soviet Union itself. Why should the Kremlin assume greater risks and costs for a modest bonus, South Africa, that would not add all that much to Moscow's global power?

In South Africa, thousands of white and millions of black people loathe the apartheid system. Are they all agents or tools of the Kremlin? Not today. But they might come to be if they are continually harassed by the authorities and accused of complicity in revolutionary violence fomented from abroad. The effect of domestic security policy based on a perception of total onslaught is to alienate still further well-meaning nonviolent critics who wish to reform what even some members of the government recognize as an antiquated system that must be changed.

In sum, the total onslaught is not total and never has been. If it were, South Africa would be more completely isolated, its trade with the rest of the world more difficult, its citizens constrained more completely in their movements around the world, and the levels of violence against the country from internal as well as external sources would multiply many times over. Is the threat real? Definitely. But it is not total, and by labelling it as such at this stage may appear at first glance to be shrewd politics, but in the longer run it detracts from the credibility of policy makers in Pretoria. It may make it virtually impossible to increase the dosage of motivation and mobilization later.

This much has virtually been admitted. Although by no means accepting that the threat has been diminished in any way, *Paratus*, an official SADF monthly, editorialized: "Like a coin whose value-imprint becomes obscured by excessive handling, the term 'total onslaught' has lost currency because some people feel that it has been overexposed and overused."[25] This being said, *Paratus* went on to detail its image of Soviet activities against South Africa and to call for vigilance and resistance to the "total onslaught."

More common is the assertion that the term is being officially played down because it has been misinterpreted. It was intended, some officials say, to depict the full extent of Soviet-inspired hostile acts, not their intensity. Those hostile to South Africa are involved in all manner of organizational activity, but they execute their policy with the greatest caution. This, Pretoria maintains, is a long-term policy, but a profound threat to the West, nevertheless.

Crucial to the maintenance of the South African regime is the necessity to devise a coordinated, wholistic, counterrevolutionary strategy. It is the mark of the present government, although it by no means originated when P. W. Botha replaced J. B. Vorster as prime minister, that "a more conscious, concerted, and systematic effort is being made to integrate various mechanisms of white control to produce a counter-revolutionary package more rationalized and efficient than at any time before."[26] P. W. Botha and his most trusted associates, particularly General Magnus Malan, had sought to fashion such a strategy during Botha's tenure as minister of defense in the Vorster government. Other political forces and personalities pursued different, though not necessarily conflicting, agendas. Since achieving leadership of the National Party and the prime ministership, however, P. W. Botha has been well positioned to formulate and implement his programs.

In practically every respect, the fascination with a coordinated "total national strategy," and consequently with the deepening involvement of the defense establishment in multifaceted aspects of civilian life, as well as in defense concerns, grows quite logically from the strategic thinking now identified with top-level SADF personnel. These views are increasingly popular in the National Party and with its voting constituents.[27]

CHAPTER II

The Growth of the Security Forces and the Evolution of Strategic Plans

I. THE RISE OF THE DEFENCE FORCES AND THE SOUTH AFRICAN POLICE

The growth in the force levels, budgets. and quantity of material and equipment (as well as their improved quality), and in the professional skills of the various coercive arms of the South African state is a matter of public record. From a cash budget of 44 million rand in 1960 to 4,722 million rand in 1985–86, the SADF's spending reflects the government's commitment to strength and military excellence.[1] Likewise, the South African Police (SAP) has seen its budgetary vote expand from R29 million to R1,618 million in those same years.[2] There is no publicly available breakdown of figures into normal policing, security, and counterinsurgency activities. Yet clearly the division of labor between SAP and SADF is quite interchangeable, especially inside South Africa. In politics, money talks. In regard to these governmental subventions, money appropriated is the product of a political process in which the individuals and institutions supporting the security establishment are well placed and appreciated by those in positions to distribute funds.

Even accounting for inflation, these are significant patterns of growth, and they have taken their toll on the economy and on taxpayers' resolve. While more and more white citizens have come to hear and heed the government's tocsin to arms, the magnitude of the cost and the personal and family sacrifices to military service are beginning to stir murmurs of dissatisfaction.

Ironically, the level of expenditure has not been particularly high in comparison to other countries in the Third World. Defense expenditures in South Africa have risen from 2.3 percent of the GNP in 1969–70 to an estimated 5.5 percent in 1977–78.[3] This proportion has declined slightly since then, to 4.2 percent by 1982.[4]

Another way of assessing the extent of budgetary commitment is to look at defense expenditure as a proportion of total state expenditure. To some extent this is a weak comparative measure among states, since in socialist states state expenditures cover a much wider range of economic and social factors. Hence, defense expenditures tend to represent a smaller proportion of the overall state budget even though, in absolute terms, they may be as large or larger than in capitalist or mixed-economy states. Likewise, unitary states with a single, centralized budget appear to spend a lower proportion of overall state expenditures than federal states or than unitary states with regional administrative subdivisions with their own separate budgets. In the United States, for example, states provide many services, including education, police and fire protection, street and road maintenance, some health and welfare services, among others. The result is that defense, exclusively a central government responsibility, appears to represent a larger share of the federal budget. To some lesser extent, South Africa has a similar arrangement.

Bearing this in mind, defense expenditures in South Africa, as indicated only by the Defence votes (without hidden expenditures in the other votes—see the following paragraph), have been falling as a proportion of state expenditures since 1977. In that year, defense consumed 18.2 percent of the total state budget. In 1981 it was 16.8 percent, and in 1985 it was down to 13.8 percent. Compared with the 1982 figures for Israel (40.7 percent), South Korea (35 percent), the United States (29.2 percent), and even Switzerland (21.4 percent), South Africa hardly looks extended.[5]

These are the sorts of arguments advanced by South African apologists to "prove" that their policies are not militaristic and that military spending has not become overly burdensome. To be sure, many other states, including some not at war or in a state of tension with neighbors, appear to devote a greater share of their national treasure to security. But Pretoria's commitment to coercive maintenance of the white power regime is not insignificant. It is important to realize that actual defense expenditures are notoriously hard to approximate reliably, and major military operations, such as Operation Askari into Angola in December 1983, force extraordinary, unpredictable budgetary calculations. Defense expenditures really consist of two related budgets—the regular approved budget and a larger "authorized" budget that enables the SADF to exceed its approved budget. Even the Defence Department admits that "the old cash budget has become obsolete."[6] More reliable is the SADF's "committal authority." Invariably the cash budget has proven inadequate in recent years. The "committal authority" is acknowledged to be the actual budget. Parliament has generally been prepared to make up the short fall. In 1982–83 that amounted to an additional R227 million, or 7.4 percent of Defence's cash budget.

SADF is also permitted to recover certain monies from the Commission for Administration for expenditures related to any improvements in conditions of service. In addition, there are security authorizations scattered and hidden in other parts of the budget—prisons, justice, the SAP, the Council for Scientific and Industrial Research, railway police, the Institute for Marine Technology, the National Intelligence Service, and the State Security votes, to name a few, and various expenditures related to Armscor and other manufacturing enterprises and services with quasi-security responsibilities. The Secret Services Account is a favorite device. In 1983–84 it received R67 million under the "Related Services" vote of the Department of Finance. This account is drawn upon by the Security Services Special Account, the State Security Council Account (which used to be under the vote of the Prime Minister's Office), the Special Defence Account, the Foreign Affairs Special Account, and the Information Special Account—and any other government department engaged in secret services. Even the Department of Community Development contributes R63.9 million (1983–84) to defense by providing buildings, structures, and land to the SADF for defense purposes and R30 million to the police and the courts.[7] No matter how it is accounted for, expansion of the security budget must follow inevitably from the panorama perceived from Pretoria.

The size and composition of the forces also reflect a determination to build a formidable security apparatus that can deter potential aggressors and dissidents as well as achieve operational effectiveness when ordered into the field.

The SADF is really two distinctive bodies. One includes the "full-time" forces, consisting of the Permanent Force of professionals or careerists and the national servicemen who are called up for two years. The latter are mostly white males doing compulsory service, but there are a number of Coloured and Asian volunteers. The second component of the SADF is the "part-time" reserve, composed of several hundred thousand Citizen Force and Commando Force members. Their units have from time to time been called up for long tours of active service, but full mobilization would be extremely costly and might well lead to economic and social collapse.

In 1960 the SADF numbered 11,500 Permanent Force and 56,500 part-time men and women (plus 10,000 national servicemen). National Service is the military obligation of all fit white male citizens. This resulted in a standing operational force of 21,500 men. By 1983, those figures had been increased to 29,300 PF, 157,000 part-timers, and 53,100 national servicemen.[8] The standing operational force by this time had reached 82,400. The SAP, because of problems of recruitment and wastage (resignation or dismissal after training but before the tour of duty has been fulfilled), numbered 37,126 members in 1983,[9] up only 31 percent since 1962.

If looked on as a proportion of men-in-arms to total population, this growth has been steady, but not especially unusual for socially heterogeneous states. But when viewed as a proportion of the white population of South Africa it is remarkable. The total complement of SADF military personnel, including Citizen Force and Commando units and national servicemen, has risen steadily since 1970. In 1970 these forces represented only 0.54 percent of the total South African population. By 1975 their proportion was up to 1.09 percent and by 1983, 1.5 percent. A not insignificant part of that apparent increase arises from the fact that South African statisticians no longer include people of the Transkei, Bophuthatswana, Venda, and the Ciskei in the population data for the Republic. But if the total SADF is viewed as a proportion of the total white population, the 1970 figure is 3.1 percent. In 1975 it was 6.5 percent. By 1983 it had jumped to 8.6 percent. The militarization of the society in this regard is undeniable. Again, however, this by no means approaches the levels of mobilization in some East European and Middle Eastern states. Israel, for example, can field 505,000 fighters in a total population of 4,100,000—fully 12.4 percent of the total population.[10]

The various amendments to the omnibus Defence Act of 1957 have, through the years, made it increasingly likely that white male citizens will be called for military service. The length of their initial and subsequent service assignments has been steadily increased as well. Initially a ballot system determined by chance who would be called. The period of service began with three months. In 1967 compulsory conscription was introduced, initially for a period of nine months. In 1972 that was raised to twelve months, and five years later national service was increased to twenty-four months. Likewise, the postinitial service obligation in the Citizen Force was raised from nineteen days a year for five years to thirty days per year for eight years in 1977. Nonetheless, SADF still occasionally requires national servicemen to serve three-month tours of duty.

In 1982 these obligations were amended again.[11] The period of further service was increased from eight to twelve years. The total service commitment was extended from 240 to 720 days beyond the initial two years. The twelve years eligibility has been divided into six two-year cycles. No one will have to serve more than ninety days per calendar year or more than 120 days per cycle in total. Even after their Citizen Force service, men are required to serve five more years as members of the Active Citizen Force Reserve. Moreover, serious efforts have been made to engage those white males under the age of sixty who have so far escaped military service. These individuals will be involved in the National Reserve, and if they have had no previous military training they may be required to serve thirty days in their first year of service and, thereafter, up to the age of fifty-five years, to serve twelve days per calendar year.

Other bodies, such as the Commandos, provide additional alternatives but the total effect of these amendments is to prepare the groundwork for a more rapid and thorough mobilization should an emergency be determined to exist.

Even noncitizens, in certain circumstances, are eligible for compulsory military service, and the acquisition of citizenship is less voluntary than before. According to 1984 legislation, all immigrants who remain in the country for five years will automatically become South African citizens, and thereby eligible for national service, unless they declare that they do not wish to be citizens. But the decision not to secure citizenship means the forfeiture (for a male between fifteen and twenty-five) of his permanent residence rights. Without such rights he cannot be legally employed. Either he leaves South Africa, or he shares the defense burden with all other South African citizens.

Each successive escalation of military service obligations and each tightening of the manpower net indicates a higher priority attached to military preparedness by the government and the preferred position of the SADF over other claimants for government protection and support. The private economy is particularly hard hit by these lengthened terms of service, as is the educational system. Family life is also complicated by repeated and unexpected call-ups. But it is the mark of white South Africa's determination to retain power that it should prefer such changed demands to other alternatives.

II. THE INCREASED USE OF BLACKS IN THE ARMED FORCES

Numbers and legal obligations alone do not tell the entire story. The changing racial composition of the armed forces signifies a realization that the security situation is regarded as serious, although not desperate.[12] It had often been stated by high-level National Party leaders, until the early 1960s, that blacks must never be armed or required to serve in combat assignments in the SADF. As late as 1970 the minister of defense had stated that black Africans would be employed by his department only as common laborers. Their deployment would be solely in "traditional roles," menial positions as cooks, batmen, orderlies, laborers, drivers, and so forth. Despite their expressed aversion to arming blacks, in 1963 the SADF was authorized to reestablish the Coloured Corps. Ten years later a black African unit was created (now known as the 21 Battalion), and later still, in 1979, a number of ethnic-cum-regional formations were established to be attached to various regional commands.

By early 1983 the SADF had an estimated ten thousand black (Coloured, Indian, and black African) members. This figure does not include the various armies and national guards now attached to the "independent national states" or homelands, the black members of the SWATF, the South West African Territorial Force, (a significant proportion of that force), or the blacks in paramilitary formations of the SAP. But the black forces in the SADF itself constitute around a third of the Army and Navy PF. Seen in this context, the black contribution to the career Defence Force is noteworthy, especially the changeover in the past few years. But, by including Air Force PF numbers, the black proportion falls to 22 percent of the PF. Dilution is far greater when one adds white national servicemen and still further when Citizen Force and Commando units are considered. Black units, however, have been actively involved in border patrols, cross-border operations, and combat duties in the operational areas. Factor in blacks in the Namibian forces and blacks in military and paramilitary police formations deployed in the operational area, and recently units of the "independent national states" armies have been to the operational area, and one can see that blacks bear a disproportionate burden of combat (compared to their numbers in the SADF itself). The 32 Battalion (composed mostly of Portuguese-speaking blacks from Angola and chiefly assigned to cross-border strikes), the SAP COIN units (mostly Ovambo) noted for their tracking tenacity within Namibia, and various San units alone must account for an extremely high proportion of contacts with SWAPO, the South West African Peoples Organization.[13] In this sense, blacks can be regarded as a form of "cannon fodder," as alleged by the African National Congress.[14] In that blacks are volunteers this argument may be less compelling. But there is an "economic draft" of sorts, forcing young blacks out of the private economy that holds little promise into a *relatively* well-paid and secure "job"in the SADF. So far, most of the published reports on blacks in the SADF indicate that these men have obediently and efficiently performed their assigned duties.

With the new political dispensation that assigns a direct role for Coloured and Asian citizens in politics and central government institutions, quite expectedly there is talk about extending obligatory national service to include young males from these population groups. If they secure the same political rights as whites (which is doubtful), why should they not carry the same responsibilities, runs the argument.[15] Although there has been a steady expansion of the use of Coloured men (a 22 percent increase in their numbers from 1982 to 1984), Asians in the SADF have not increased.[16] It appears that, despite representation from the South African Cape Corps Ex-Servicemen's Legion in favor of two years compulsory national service for all Coloured males over the age of seventeen, most Coloureds oppose the idea at the present time.[17]

The Coloured Labour Party, which had earlier supported the constitutional referendum at its 1984 congress, refused to endorse conscription of Coloured people.[18] For its part, government contends that as long as there are more Coloured volunteers than can be accommodated by the SADF, it has no intention of extending compulsory national service to that population group.[19] Presumably, however, it is a matter of time and money before government reconsiders the question seriously.

Government's overall view is unmistakable, and is probably based on an undeniable reality (although their time frame may be exaggerated). Their view, predicated as it is on the twin concepts of "total onslaught" and "total national strategy," is that the next five years will be decisive, and that "if we want to survive" the Defence Force must be enlarged and strengthened.[20] Since the source of white manpower has already been overextended, a further increase of the full-time force can only be brought about by involving larger numbers of other population groups.[21] This view, of course, is not shared officially by the Conservative Party and the Herstigte Nasionale Party. Dr. Ferdie Hartzenberg, former Cabinet minister and now chairman of the CP's executive committee, calls for a return to apartheid in all walks of life. This includes separate defense forces with separate uniforms for each "nation" in South Africa.[22] Greater involvement of all race groups in a single SADF has been, however, strongly endorsed by the Progressive Federal Party (PFP). One PFP spokesman likened South Africa's situation to that of Lebanon, in which different groups had different armies, and the result "has been disastrous." In that regard he rejected the CP model.[23]

The speed and ease with which the white community came to accept the employment of blacks in the SADF in combat assignments is remarkable. In less than a decade white public opinion has been largely transformed from opposing the arming of blacks to encouraging a wider use of black units, albeit in essentially segregated situations. The voters seem satisfied that control is retained by white officers. The step-by-step progression of phasing in and expanding the black forces has been so carefully managed that many whites originally critical of black troops have been won over or at least neutralized. Pragmatic justifications for policy changes have had their impact. Fears regarding black loyalty and efficiency no longer seem to prevent whites from acknowledging the need for forces from all race groups. Black units are accepted because the "experiment" has worked and because black fighting effectiveness has been demonstrated. But the official puffery about a "people's army," an army of all of the people, is sham and self-delusion. Few whites have any intention of supporting a military structure with blacks in proportionate or even significant positions of authority and command.

III. THE IMPORTANCE OF DOMESTIC ORDER

Other aspects of strategic thought have recently emerged. In 1982 General Constand Viljoen, the commander in chief of the SADF, talked of "total victory" in five years, and he refered not just to military victory. This will come, in his view, through efforts to reach political settlements in both South Africa and Namibia. Yet one might add that the SADF seems to be a factor delaying settlement in Namibia and has proven to be troublesome for Mozambique. In their efforts to secure a virtually risk-free Namibian settlement ushering to power elements that would coop- erate with South Africa, and in their hopes to deliver a "knock-out" blow in the war effort, (one that they hope might negate the need to negotiate at all with SWAPO), SADF advisors have resisted significant compromise. They seem to be saying that time is really on their side. By 1987 Africans "will eventually see through the intentions of Russia."[24] Why official SADF sources have fastened on a five-year span in what clearly is a protracted political-military war of attrition is not clear. It almost invites second-guessing. In the past, SADF leaders have not been noted for an overly optimistic or naive perspective.

These views reflect, as well, a kind of juggling act being performed by South Africa's strategic thinkers. They do not neglect the regional strategic picture, and much of their discussion revolves around Namibian settle- ment that politically would not undermine the Botha government and its white constituencies in the Republic and Namibia and would not, in the opinion of SADF headquarters, leave South Africa militarily exposed. If not friendly, then at least not actively hostile governments must be in place and the government hopes firmly so in the "national states," or homelands, and among the Republic's immediate neighbors. For geo- political reasons, measured criticism and even hostility can be tolerated more in some states than in others. Such matters as well as strategic cooperation and coordination will be discussed in chapters 5 and 6.

The SADF at the behest of the government has started to pay more systematic attention to domestic or internal security concerns. This can be seen in the emphases of the Defence Department in its latest strategic "line" and in its legislative proposals. Not that the SADF and government have abandoned the international aspects of security and border defense. Rather these concerns are now supplemented by a reemphasis on pre- venting and combatting internal unrest. Domestic internal security has long been a theme of successive South African governments. But generally it had been a concern of departments normally identified with domestic issues—Justice, Police, Bantu Affairs, Internal Affairs, and so forth. It is significant that the Department of Defence and the SADF as its operational arm have now taken up the matter. Of course, internal security has always been important to the SADF, from the time of the "Rebellion" of 1914 and the 1922 miners' strike and operations against recalcitrant black peoples. According to the Defence Act of 1957 as amended, the second function of the SADF is to be employed "on service in the prevention or suppression of internal disorder in the Republic."[25] But in the past it had been generally assumed that this was clearly a secondary function. It still may be so, but recent utterances and troop deployments in the townships indicate that the SADF is increasingly aware that when the security of the state is at stake, defensive and domestic security considerations overlap—they cannot be kept separate.

In at least three ways, changes in strategic thinking point up a new concentration on domestic stability. First is a studious attention to urban unrest. Jonathan Kapstein, a close observer of South Africa, indicates that South African military strategists use as "their bible" the writings of French Legionnaire officer Roger Trinquier. From his Algerian experience, Trinquier argues that it is possible to control urban opposition from a technical and tactical viewpoint.[26] Aware that it would be expensive if not impossible to fight both an external and an internal war at the same time, SADF thinkers have urged domestic political, economic, and social reforms to defuse a polarized and tense situation. On the basis of the British experience in Malaysia and the French example in Algeria, some military spokesmen believe that managed social change can be an instrument to weaken or reduce the appeal of revolutionary movements. The carrot and the stick are to be used in tandem.

The repeated 20 percent military/80 percent political solution comes to mind. According to this view the struggle for South Africa is principally a political and social contest. The military hierarchy claims to be concerned chiefly with providing the politicians with the time and secure environment to bring about the needed changes. "It is at most a 20 percent military struggle as opposed to an 80 percent political, economic and social struggle," Brigadier Ben Roos, then Director of Army Operations, stated.[27] The axiomatic 80/20 ratio is shared by the PFP's former spokesman on defense, Harry Schwarz, and by the NRP defense specialist W. Vause Raw, journalists, commentators, and ordinary citizens.[28] General Malan asserts: "Militarily we can win the war. We can win it tomorrow. But this is the type of battle you never win on the military field. You win it in the political field." [29] It might be asked in all seriousness, what are the politicians doing to assure that military pressures will eventually be relieved? Will the new constitutional design, which neglects in its essentials the black 70 percent of the population, satisfy the black leaders and citizenry? The answer is an emphatic no.

To achieve domestic tranquility, SADF personnel can increasingly be found deployed within South Africa, far from the Republic's borders. These include Civic Action schoolteachers in Soweto, medical teams in the homelands, and SADF units cordoning off townships during SAP swoops or SADF troops manning roadblocks. Civic Action is a branch of the SADF involved in governmental service functions largely as a form of psychological warfare. The formerly low profile of the SADF domestically has been raised and activated.

IV. THE CONCEPT OF "AREA DEFENCE"

After a renewed interest in urban unrest comes a number of references to what is called a "second front." General Malan in 1982 interpreted a series of bomb attacks in Cape Town, the eastern Transvaal, Natal, and Soweto as a "second front."[30] By this he meant a preconventional warfare strategy that includes an increase of sabotage strikes against selected, largely symbolic targets. Despite the fact that the minister of law and order rejects calling these strikes "armed propaganda," it appears that the SADF and the Defence Department acknowledge the largely political and symbolic purposes they serve. The impression was that such unrest was growing with 12 incidents reported in 1979, 19 in 1980, and 55 in 1981. Between January 1977 and October 1982, Tom Lodge was able to identify at least 150 discrete violent acts apparently inspired or carried out by the ANC. He noted 33 incidents of sabotage of railway communications, 25 attacks on industrial installations, 35 attacks on individuals (including assassinations), 19 clashes between police or army units and insurgents, 15 bombings, 14 attacks on administrative buildings, 13 against police stations, and 3 against military targets.[31] Although the number of incidents in 1982 fell to 32, many were designed for high propaganda impact. This trend to high visibility violence continued in 1983 and 1984 as the ANC was pushed farther from the borders and found itself in need of regrouping, reorganization, and the image of vitality. Moreover, revolutionary operatives have demonstrated greater efficiency than in the past.

Thus South Africa wants to be prepared for both sorts of warfare— conventional assaults when conventional defenses are lowered, and sabotage behind the "lines" for psychological, propaganda, and political effect. The second front far from Namibia and inside the Republic's borders also serves to spread the security forces thin. According to General Viljoen, ANC politicization of the black community has not gone far enough to support revolutionary action. But to undermine a reformist "political solution," revolutionaries are expected to step up sabotage and subversion. Viljoen thinks that the ANC operates without popular support, and therefore their isolated strikes seek "to create an atmosphere of instability while endeavoring to get maximum publicity from the least activity."[32]

The government has responded by coining the concept of "area defence" and fashioning call-up policy to satisfy such needs. Unlike SWAPO, the enemy fighting Pretoria does not plan a "border war" but rather an "area war." To contend with this, "people living in an area must be organized to defend themselves." They are the first line of defense. The full-time SADF then becomes a "reaction force." In theory the armed citizenry, or large segments of it, are expected to bear the primary responsibility for containing localized outbreaks of violence. In reality, the professionals are still paramount.

The Defence Department sought to have the Defence Act amended during the 1982 session of Parliament to be able to call on a large reservoir of auxiliary manpower "so that no area in SA will be vulnerable to attack."[33] The act does not foreshadow "total mobilisation," but rather is designed as a contingency measure. The object of the Defence Amendment Act of 1982 is not to call up all eligible men to the age of fifty-five. That would be impossible and impractical anyway. Rather, the purpose is to be legislatively empowered to do so in selected areas that are under attack or infiltration. Area defense, if it means anything, necessitates that the SADF take advantage of a specialized knowledge of the terrain and people of a locality. Local farmers, in particular, seem well suited to provide such intelligence and field skills. Thus it would appear that the Defence Amendment Act is not fashioned to swell the ranks of the Defence Force across the board, but to call upon eligible men in selected locales or with particular skills as the need arises.[34] There is the further possibility that SADF might use the compulsory service provisions of the Defence Amendment Act to provide staff for civil (as opposed to military) service departments with staff shortages.[35] To sharpen local defense structures, the territorial command structure was also reorganized and decentralized in 1983. The extensive North Transvaal Command was divided into three regional commands: North Transvaal, East Transvaal, and Pretoria.[36]

V. FURTHER ISSUES OF DOMESTIC SECURITY AND DEFENSE

Other legislation also focuses on domestic security questions. One might cite a battery of laws passed to inhibit publication or dissemination of information regarding the activities of the police and other security forces. Between 1977 and 1981 more than twelve statutes were enacted to this end,[37] many of which placed the burden of proof that there be "reasonable grounds" for their reports on the accused, that is, the publisher. The affect has been to stifle reports that show the SADF and the police in a bad light.

More directly, the National Key Points Act of 1980 gives the minister of defense extensive authority to declare any premises a National Key Point. Thus, "any place or area [that] is so important that its loss, damage, disruption or immobilization may prejudice the Republic" may be so designated. The owners thereby are obligated to undertake security precautions, such as storing weapons and communications equipment, and organizing and training a defense unit to secure the Key Point against "terroristic activities, sabotage, espionage or subversion."[38] Failure to comply with these regulations could entail a fine of R20,000. In return, the companies would be offered financial incentives, including tax concessions, when they purchase weapons and other security equipment and when they train security staff. Ironically, there is some question whether a subsidiary of a foreign firm is permitted to inform its home office of its security plans and of expenditures related to security, and even whether the firm has been declared a Key Point.[39]

Although it took some time for the act to be put into force, it is believed that as of 1984, some 413 sites have been classified as Key Points. They include airports, power stations, oil refineries, and chemical plants.[40] In addition there are hundreds of other locations known as "important places." A National Key Points Committee was constituted by the minister in November 1980 to implement the act. It is chaired by the chief director of operations in the SADF and includes other high ranking SADF personnel, plus the administrator of the Transvaal, the commissioners of the SAP and the Railway Police, the postmaster general, and top ranking officials from the NIS, the Departments of Industries, Commerce and Tourism, and Mineral and Energy Affairs. The actual instructions and regulations relating to the act were not published until November 1982. The SADF has demonstrated some flexibility in providing courses for "industrial commandos," voluntary employee units on site to protect industrial installations.[41] At some sites the firm provides security in-house or by contracting with a private security firm, a number of which have been formed. Security has become a multimillion rand business with an estimated turnover of around R600 million in 1983.[42]

In border areas of South Africa farms are being abandoned, and isolated rural communities are vulnerable to violence.[43] Recent efforts to improve security there likewise point up a concern with the psychological as well as military dimensions of the problem. The Departments of Agriculture and of Defence are anxious to avoid white depopulation of the platteland. Yet in 1982, 40 percent of the Transvaal farms along the border from Mozambique to Botswana no longer had white resident farmers. Most of those remaining are heavily armed and are digging in behind security fencing. Many farmers are leaving, but generally not for security reasons. Rather the economic future for them is bleak. Drought, high costs, labor shortages, and poor infrastructure are the key reasons. Almost all feel that terrorism will increase. The Density of the Population in Designated Areas Act, passed in 1979, is supposed to offer low interest loans to farmers who move to or stay in demarcated areas. Not until 1983 were regulations drafted for this program. According to certain sections of the act, the minister of agriculture is empowered to prevent farmers from leaving border farms. Absentee landowners are required to provide effective white occupancy to bushveld farms along a strip ten to twenty kilometers wide along the Limpopo River, if the farms are sold after May 1983. However, the government's previous financial assistance program for border farmers failed for lack of funds.[44] Agricultural subsidies are costly and don't necessarily keep farmers on unproductive land. Ideas to purchase abandoned farms have been bruited about among defense planners, and resettling demobilized national servicemen on such farms has been suggested. The proposal of a "ring of steel" around the borders to provide protection for outlying areas is popular in defense circles, for both South Africa and Namibia. The plan was suggested to establish a series of fortified strong points linked into a radio network.[45] Cactus fences topped by barbed wire and razor wire fences are being erected, too. But localized vulnerabilities are still apparent.

VI. THE THEME OF CONVENTIONAL WAR

The South African Army is divided into two main operational wings—a counterinsurgency force (COIN) and a conventional force. For the past decade or more emphasis has been placed on building COIN capacity. This force is charged with maintaining internal security, "area defence," and with preventing border infiltrations. As such, most reserve or part-time soldiers have been trained or retrained for COIN duties. In the 1982 defense white paper, destabilization, subversion, indirect onslaught, and insurgency were the watchwords, although there were hints that conventional warfare might be possible. Total onslaught by its nature highlighted hostile nonmilitary activities, and military struggle arrived in the form of low-level terrorism. "It is the aim of the USSR to tie down the SA Defence Force by means of a protracted terrorist war in SWA, while at the same time giving increased assistance to terrorist action in the RSA."[46] This white paper excerpt set the tone for strategic thinking in Pretoria.

Yet the conventional war theme, long muted or dormant, began again to be played by SADF planners in late 1983 and early 1984. Pointing to the increasing supply of weapons and military equipment to Angola from

the Soviet bloc (some R10 billion from 1978 to 1983), and to the expansion
of ground forces in neighboring states (around 300 percent increase since
1977), General Viljoen and others now warn of a conventional assault on
South Africa.[47] The nonaggression pact with Mozambique and the cease-
fire with Angola could serve to deflect and delay the guerrilla struggle
against Namibia and South Africa. With the isolation of the ANC and
SWAPO forces, the prospect of conventional threat takes on a different
meaning. "The development of the conventional threat against the RSA,"
says the 1984 defense white paper

> will be continuously influenced by the extent and intensity of the USSR arms
> support programme in Southern Africa. Owing to several factors certain states
> in Southern Africa do not constitute an immediate conventional threat to the
> RSA. However, a conventional threat does exist due to the fact that the
> USSR, through its sustained supply of advanced armaments and personnel
> to these states, is disturbing the military balance in respect of the availability
> of military equipment in Southern Africa.[48]

In response, South Africa is urged to "concentrate on the development,
production and commissioning of a new generation of main armaments
in order to meet the threat of the Soviet arms stockpile in certain neighboring countries and to maintain the existing balance of power."[49] Deterrence, conventional onslaught, arms development, and buildup are
the watchwords in Pretoria since the diplomatic breakthroughs.

Such defensive schemes themselves, and vacillation between strategic
themes, are a reflection of the times—of South Africa's shrinking hinter-
land, of the southward movement of the defense perimeter of the Republic
from the Equator, to the Zambezi, to the Cunene, to the Limpopo and
eventually to the Orange, to an indistinct and nebulous locale that is
everywhere and nowhere. The government is not yet prepared to adopt
a counsel of last resort. Foreign policy and expansive security plans still
are central to the defense of the order. South African strategy reflects,
however, an awareness of the need for a complete and wholistic security
system. There is in South Africa a confluence of interests between today's
NP politicians in government, the SADF, and the various intelligence
services. All of them see and believe that the communist menace is not
only real, but the most profound challenge to their system and their rule.
Since the immediate communist challenge is perceived to be military and
to be largely based beyond South Africa's borders and those of Namibia,
then the immediate response is military and offensively oriented. Thus
General Viljoen can say that he believes in "offensive defense." "You
have to be aggressive, as this demonstrates your determination."[50] A
baffling bit of Orwellian newspeak appears in the 1982 White Paper,

where it is written that if circumstances demand it, the SADF will engage in "offensive pro-active action."[51]

Likewise, security schemes include the creation of a constellation of southern African states and collaboration among neighboring "national states" in preventing Marxist incursions. Physical and material policies also demonstrate that these foreign factors will not be neglected. But of late there have been shifts in the stresses of security rhetoric, themselves an outgrowth of perceived menace. These are additional themes joined to an already immense commitment to regional defense. Yet regional defense does not necessarily represent a commitment to regional stability. Stability serves a political purpose provided it is marked by certain kinds of governments with acceptable foreign policies in the right ideological mode. I shall deal with many of these ideas later.

CHAPTER III

Centralization of State Power and the Centrality of the Security Establishment

I. GOVERNMENT RATIONALIZATION

Those who study South Africa can perceive certain shifts in the institutional setting and center of gravity for high-level policymaking. In each of these shifts, the security establishment and especially the defense services have gained influence at the expense of other bodies. Before trying to describe the nature of these changes, it will be helpful to place them in a more narrow idiosyncratic context. In other words, experiences of the key actors have contributed to shaping the trends that are reflected in the institutions and roles involved. To many, what will be written here is conventional wisdom, but scholars have a capacity for neglecting the obvious in their analyses. Some consciously deny a consideration of personal data about role occupants altogether. They argue that personalities are a product of larger cultural or economic or institutional factors. In the most general sense that view is not farfetched.[1] But to accept it completely may lead to rejecting a source of data rich in explanatory power and suggestive of insights otherwise lost in the "big picture."

P. W. Botha personally has been responsible for so many of the changes that have been undertaken. His leadership style is considerably different from that of his predecessor. And his principal governmental experience as minister of defense accounts in large part for the phenomena described in this study. To begin with, P. W. Botha is a manager, an organizational virtuoso, a leader who relies on expert advice, planning, preparation, structure, and follow-through. He is, as one academic put it, a "forceful managing director." This contrasts with John Vorster's "chairman of the board" style.[2] Where Vorster's lead was slack, Botha's is firm. With consummate political and administrative skill Botha seized the reins of government, not without challenge. From time to time he has been forced to slow the pace of executive consolidation, to modify his policies, and even to retreat in the face of vocal and concerted opposition. But the trend is unmistakable—government is being enlarged, centralized, and streamlined. Efficiency and performance matter, and it is increasingly difficult for independent centers of power to become entrenched.

The overall process has been characterized by what is called the "rationalization" of the government and the public service. This entails, inter alia, the centralization of power at several levels, much different from the ad hoc approach to government characterized by Vorster and H. F. Verwoerd. Disclosures stemming from the information scandal from 1974 to 1978 reveal much about Vorster's leadership. The scandal itself grew out of a slovenly administrative and decisional style marked by departmental autonomy and debilitating interdepartmental political competition. Revelations of illegal or suspect practices hit close to Vorster. His supervision of state was, at best, loose. Vorster's rule, in retrospect, was an organizational and administrative nightmare in more ways than one.

To correct this, Botha has simultaneously reorganized the cabinet, developed an interlocking and focused system of cabinet committees to devise and propose policy and coordinate its implementation, engaged and broadened the scope of the office of the prime minister, launched a President's Council charged with the monumental task of advising government on constitutional development and racial relations, and embarked on a difficult, controversial, and potentially momentous reconstitution of the South African polity, including a new constitution and new parliamentary/executive structures. These organizational changes were started in earnest in September 1979, when the prime minister combined a score of established cabinet committees into five major committees. Some had been only paper committees. Others had met but sporadically, and possessed at best fuzzy charges. P. W. Botha gave them clear assignments, saw to it that they met periodically, and coordinated and regularized their procedures.[3]

The various layers of executive government have loosely parallel structures. But several conclusions are self-evident. Decision making at the top has been tightened and centralized. P.W. Botha is indispensible to the process and, in large measure thanks to him, the security establishment exercises an enlarged role. Policy decisions are more likely to be enforced and implemented than in the past, with interdepartmental coordination the norm rather than the exception. Make no mistake, the bureaucracy is still a bureaucracy , with all the built-in institutional and personal features of conscious delay, resistance, inefficiency, and error. Botha may be relatively efficient and professional, but he still must move a massive governmental machine that sometimes drags its feet, or worse. But in comparison with the past, the managerial revolution has arrived in Pretoria, and the vanguard of that revolution has been P. W. and "his" SADF.

II. RELIANCE ON DEFENSE SPECIALISTS

To a large extent these managerial reforms reflect P. W. Botha's own personality. Throughout his career he has been an organization man, a manager.[4] He rose to prominence as a party careerist, identified for years with the cadre of the Cape branch of the National Party, where he gained a reputation as a brilliant organizer and administrator. In April 1966 he was appointed minister of defense, a post he held until 1980. Although it is hard to say who influenced whom, it is apparent that Botha presided over the modernization and enlargement of the SADF. The professional military technocrats he admired and promoted in the SADF, in turn, taught Botha some lessons about managerial efficiency, planning, professionalism, and hierarchical organizations. The cross-fertilization process has been salutary for both the armed forces and for Botha's maturation as an executive. Thus a large part of the explanation for the rise of the defense establishment in governmental circles is the fact that during his tenure as minister, Botha was able to identify and elevate officers of intellectual and administrative promise. Botha's association with General Malan is the most notable. In rapid succession Botha appointed Malan chief of staff of the army, chief of the army, and chief of the SADF, in each instance the youngest ever to occupy those positions. Then in 1980 Botha named Malan to succeed him as minister of defense. There is a special trust between the two men, and the prime minister clearly relies on the general for advice on strategic matters, as well as on a number of domestic political issues. Malan has not, as yet, proven to be a dominant force in parliamentary or intraparty politics. Botha's long association with the SADF has also enabled him to identify talented administrators and thinkers in "his" ministry. Thus it was natural that on becoming prime minister he should turn to individuals whose skills he had already observed first hand, or who share his perspectives.

Running throughout this account of civil-military relations are references to the close personal and professional bonds between the prime minister and particular SADF officers. There is no question that this is a classic patron-client relationship based on the twin factors of shared political support and protection, and an overall concurrence on political-strategic perceptions of the need for pragmatism and rationality in mobilizing the state's resources. It is equally understandable that, as Botha becomes engaged in the detailed affairs of other departments, he will come to recognize individual talents outside the SADF (as he has already within the Party) and to move these individuals into more responsible positions in his government, thereby in effect diluting SADF influence.

So it is no accident and no apparent conspiracy that catapulted high-ranking SADF men into political and advisory positions close to the prime minister. There SADF personnel have an advantage in the definition of social issues and the establishment of the government's agenda. The challenge of "total onslaught" is superficially a military problem. Those who view it as such quite comfortably turn to the military for guidance. In effect, the SADF are experts in control and the exercise of coercion, but not normally experts on political matters. Botha has ideas of his own. The SADF are specialists in the planning process and the execution of policy. As such they have been drawn into affairs of state outside their normal portfolio. By demonstrating certain technical-managerial skills, the SADF is involved at high levels. Much like the computer programmer or the systems analyst who, by virtue of his technical training, may take up work for an economic planner while knowing little about economics, the military planner may find himself recruited to help with the political process in education or homelands consolidation or industrial decentral-ization, among other things.

Botha has been a leader anxious to have expert input into decisions and policy execution. This contributes to an enlarged role, not just for the military elite, but for top-level civil servants and public officials—and even to involvement for specialists in private industry, the univer-sities, and the independent think tanks. To the frustration of politicians outside the inner circle and others with narrow regional bases, it has become in many ways government by professionals. One should not, however, exaggerate the extent of professionalism and efficiency. These qualities exist only in relation to predecessor governments. A cumbersome bureaucracy and irrational and inefficient behavior still dog the Botha regime.

Experts to provide counsel understandably have been resisted and resented by the rank-and-file career administrative cadre. They have not always promptly and dutifully implemented decisions taken by Botha and his associates, especially when such decisions involve the downgrading of a particular office or function or changing already familiar routines. The maxim, "the expert should be on tap, not on top," still applies. But in some fields, such as the economy and domestic security, the authorities have permitted specialists to determine the agenda and to formulate the alternatives. Because the coopted experts have demonstrated their loyalty to Botha or because they already share the perspectives of important political leaders, they have been able to make themselves indispensable.

III. RISE OF THE "EXECUTIVE STATE"

This centralization of executive power in the cabinet and particularly in a few departments, an inner circle or inner cabinet as it has been called, grows out of a personal hierarchical approach to management, as opposed to a representative mode marked by compromise, consensus, and delay. Personalized though it may be in its South African garb, it is a phenomenon common to many Western democracies.

Particularly in the area of security policy, this restructuring of the policy machinery is widespread. In the United States, for example, the need for administrative integration has demanded more than departmental advocacy and competition. Consequently, recent presidents have placed more emphasis on their National Security Council and the national security advisor. In this way, matters of defense, intelligence, and diplomacy can be better coordinated. At its press conference in September 1983, the State Security Council of South Africa preferred to compare itself to the National Security Council of the United States. In fact, the SSC is better managed and more effective as a policy-making and coordinating tool. There is still a great deal of competition and "freelancing" among its various participants, but far less than in the American context. In the words of Zbigniew Brzezinski, formerly the assistant to the president for national security affairs, the United States has, in effect, "a chaotic non-system."[5] No one today would characterize the executive structure in Pretoria as "chaotic" or unsystematic.

The rise of the "executive state" in South Africa in turn has meant the decline of two institutions representative of the exclusive white community—the National Party and Parliament. Government from above, especially when it seeks to fashion policies likely to be unpopular with one's narrow and privileged constituency, has led to a paternalistic, centralist regime, a departure from the casual "democracy for the Herrenvolk," as it was once described by Pierre van den Berghe.[6] Among rightwing Afrikaners Botha is accused of erecting, especially with the present executive presidency, a *verligte* (enlightened, or ideologically flexible) dictatorship. Other institutions too have gained or lost power and influence in the movement toward the executive state, some within the executive branch. The Department of Foreign Affairs seemed, before the Nkomati accord, to have fallen on hard times. The Information Department has been downgraded (now merged into Foreign Affairs), as has what once had been called Bantu Affairs (now the Department of Cooperation and Development), as well as the intelligence organ formerly known as BOSS and then DONS and now called the National Intelligence Service (NIS). Institutions so sloppily managed that autonomy and individuality led to embarrassment or worse and organizations with less than cost-effective procedures and structures have been marked for reorganization, reduction, or dismantlement.

IV. THE NEW CONSTITUTIONAL DISPENSATION

How will these trends toward governmental centralization and executive power be affected by the implementation of the new constitution? More specifically, will the elaborate security management system so painstakingly molded by P. W. Botha need to be substantially modified to conform to the new constitutional dispensation?

In order to answer these questions it is necessary to outline the proposed arrangements and how they are likely to work. A three-chambered legislature is composed of: a House of Assembly of 178 members representing 4.5 million whites; a House of Representatives of 85 members for the 2.5 million Coloureds; and a 45-member House of Delegates for the 800,000 Asians. A 4:2:1 ratio is thereby entrenched. The 21 million blacks are not represented at all. Each house will legislate exclusively for the "own affairs" of its racial community. Each will also be consulted on matters of "general affairs," such as foreign policy. In cases of dispute as to what is "general" and what is "own" affairs, the state president will adjudicate. Contact between the three houses is through a series of joint standing committees for "general affairs." There is still considerable confusion as to how they will function and how opposition parties will operate in these committees, if at all.

Overseeing the entire operation is the executive state president. The old office of prime minister is abolished. The state president is elected by an electoral college consisting of 50 whites, 25 Coloureds, and 13 Asians, in other words, effectively by the dominant party in the white House of Assembly. The executive president will take the lead in resolving disputes between the three chambers, normally by referring the issue to the President's Council, an advisory body of 60 members—20 elected by the white chamber, 10 by the Coloured representatives, and 5 by the Asians, plus 25 members appointed by the president. On disputes among chambers, the President's Council's decisions will be final and beyond appeal to the courts.

Government itself consists of an appointed cabinet selected by the president. This is slated to include Coloured and Asian members (at present one of each), thereby breaking with South African tradition. Each chamber has a Ministers Council for its own community affairs.

On 5 May, 1983 the new constitution was introduced in Parliament and in November it was placed in referendum before the white electorate.

Both the PFP and the rightist Conservative Party urged a "no" vote. The PFP opposed the fact that Africans were not consulted on or to be represented in the new arrangements; the Conservatives objected to any representation for Coloureds and Asians, thereby destroying the principle of exclusive separation of power and white control of the central government. Neither Coloureds nor Asians were asked to participate in the referendum. Presumably their rejection or endorsement of the constitution was reflected in their voting behavior for their separate Houses in August 1984. Some 66 percent of the white voters approved the constitution and a pleased National Party began the detailed countdown for placing the new constitution into force by late 1984. But only 30 percent of the eligible Coloureds and 20 percent of the eligible Asians troubled to vote. The NP government claims that because of intimidation from militants, ignorance, and general apathy many stayed away from the polls, and thus these figures represent sufficient support for the new constitution.

Just how will the security management system dovetail or necessitate change as the constitution evolves? Generally, the changes are perfectly compatible with the evolving security system. One student, citing the well-informed military correspondent of the *Cape Times*, claims that the initiative for the current constitutional proposals came from SADF planning as far back as 1978.[7] The implication is that this was done to justify call-up for Coloured and Indian youth—a manpower issue. More likely, constitutional revision involves the ever larger issues of political structure and executive authority and would not turn on the questionable argument that the SADF needs to expand its ranks. A strong executive president as envisioned in the constitution will legitimize the behavior of the last prime minister, in fact the same person, P. W. Botha. Indeed, parliamentary democracy has been fairly watered down in the past five years or so. The potential for authoritarian executive leadership is greater now than before. In this sense, the criticisms of the Conservative Party have been incisive. Presumably a centralized security management system under a State Security Council dominated by military leaders need not be altered in the new order. It can easily evolve into a secretariat for the state president, especially in that the new cabinet will find its role ambiguous and the parliament's roles are unclear. A cabinet with Coloured and Asian members is unlikely to be brought into the most sensitive security issues, especially if they are defined in terms of the maintenance of white power. Will Coloureds and Asians be included in the SSC? Will the SSC's decisions be put before the mixed-race cabinet? If so, will the cabinet be given the full data to discuss critically these matters? Certainly if government members have in the past said that the white opposition parties cannot be trusted with security information, would they be any more likely to share that information with Coloured and Asian ministers?

And will Coloured and Asian cabinet members be free to share security data with their own party caucuses?[8] One cannot imagine P. W. Botha and his lieutenants undermining white power by getting into foolish structural binds of their own design. More than likely, they already have in their mind's eye or even more concretely a security management system to replace the old one, and probably not significantly different from the old one. The new dispensation fits well into their model of executive government for a dynamic defense of the status quo.

V. THE SECURITY ESTABLISHMENT

The security establishment is the aggregation of institutions and groups that have a professional interest in maintaining the state. It can be divided into six identifiable components, although there is some overlap of function and membership. First and most salient are the SADF and the Department of Defence, and principally those Permanent Force officers charged with developing overall defense strategy and especially with applying it in Namibia and Angola. Reference has already been made to the growing force levels of the SADF in many of its formations. Particularly important to the present discussion are those elements of SADF responsible for tasks with strategic and political overtones. Here I include the various service academies and specialized advanced training institutes, the planning and especially strategic planning groups, Civic Action arms, intelligence and, as will become apparent shortly, those segments of the SADF that liaise regularly with governmental, political, and business elites in agencies such as the State Security Council and the Defence Manpower Liaison Committee.

The hierarchy of the SADF at the policy-making level is fairly straightforward. The chiefs of the four services (Army, Navy, Air Force, and Medical Service) report to the chief of the Defence Force, Lt. Gen Jannie Geldenhuys. General Geldenhuys assumed that position in November 1985, succeeding General Constand Viljoen, who held that post since September 1980. Now General Geldenhuys, who is also the head of the Department of Defence, is responsible to Minister of Defense Magnus Malan.

Other Defence Force institutions specialize in high-level training and in the generation of strategic ideas.[9] At an academic level is the Military Academy at Saldanha Bay. Degrees are awarded by the Faculty of Military Science of the University of Stellenbosch. If there is an intellectual elite in the SADF, Saldanha Bay produces it. Candidates for study there are carefully screened, and only the reliable survive its regimen.

The South African Joint Defence College in Pretoria also trains selected middle level and upwardly mobile officers for senior command and staff assignments. Senior government officials and private persons interested in security may also attend. The college's syllabus includes intensive study of military strategy, theory of national politics and security, as well as more practical subjects. It brings in a diverse group of non-SADF guest lecturers, by no means just those who agree with government or the SADF brass, and helps to link diverse segments of South Africa's elites.

In the Defence Headquarters, Pretoria, is the planning subdivision of the operations division. Since its establishment in 1977, it has been charged with defining the SADF's role in national strategy, with formulating coordinated strategies involving various governmental departments, and with undertaking and supporting strategic research.

The second component of the security establishment is the intelligence community. Presently it consists of the Military Intelligence Section of the SADF (MIS), the NIS (successor to BOSS), and the Security Police. Relationships among these three groups and with other governmental and political bodies have been in continual flux.[10] Each is represented on the State Security Council.

In the early 1960s, South African authorities were alarmed by the threat posed by banned organizations such as ANC, PAC, Poqo, Umkonto we Sizwe, the Communist Party, and other resistance movements. John Vorster as minister of justice and his commissioner of police felt the need for a sophisticated intelligence organization that could gather and evaluate information and thereby relieve the burden that was borne by the Security Police. Republican Intelligence (RI) was founded as a clandestine extension of the Security Police. Its members were handpicked and included the present commissioner of police and his predecessor. Their leader was then head of the Security Police, Colonel Hendrik van den Bergh, a Vorster nominee approved by Prime Minister Verwoerd. The colonel saw RI as his personal vehicle to greater power. As RI grew, it was modelled on America's CIA. But the CIA is involved largely with foreign espionage and intelligence analysis. The RI also was engaged in domestic spying, and so it also borrowed from the FBI and from MI6, the British counterpart of the CIA.

Van den Bergh's reputation flourished as RI's grew, and his close personal ties to Vorster (they had been interned together during World War II) enhanced his influence. This friendship was later to shape the nature of BOSS in the Vorster years. In 1969 the Bureau for State Security was created as a department of state, thereby bringing the wholly secret RI into the open by making its successor, BOSS, an agency with a formal, high-profile identity. But there were also smouldering resentments in security and government circles. From within BOSS came criticisms of favoritism and Broederbond domination. From the Security Police came resentment over BOSS intrusion into the Police's functions and areas of operation and over BOSS recruitment of Security Police personnel. Military Intelligence, created in 1960, suspected that van den Bergh and Vorster were plotting to have BOSS assume control of military intelligence. BOSS even had its own division responsible for military evaluation. Effectively this takeover appeared to have happened when, in 1968, General van den Bergh (he had been promoted) was appointed security advisor to the prime minister (in addition to his direction of RI). At the time this was regarded as a move to end competition between the three branches of the intelligence community. It did not. Military Intelligence bypassed van den Bergh and reported directly to Botha, as Minister of Defence; P. W., in turn, reported to the State Security Council. This led to intense rivalry between the Department of Defence and BOSS and to fierce clashes in the SSC between Botha and van der Bergh.

Rumors circulated of intra-intelligence spying, of various intelligence agencies withholding information from the others and from the security advisor, of BOSS's partisan political activities against legitimate as well as illegal political parties, and even against National Party politicians critical of van den Bergh and Vorster. Claims as well of BOSS's dirty tricks abroad were legion, but many of these were difficult to substantiate. On the other hand, Military Intelligence was, in 1972, empowered to engage in covert counterintelligence operations inside South Africa, thereby invading Security Police turf. Suspect and questionable disclosures by Arthur McGiven and Gordon Winter, former BOSS agents, have refueled speculations.[11]

BOSS grew from five hundred to over a thousand full-time employees in the decade of its existence. But van den Bergh's domination of BOSS and his symbiotic attachment to Vorster made the principal intelligence agency of state vulnerable to governmental changes at the top. The information scandal provided just the sort of predicament leading to the demise of BOSS. Like a rogue elephant BOSS had been brought down, and when the personalities that dominated it fell from grace, BOSS lost its flimsy supports.

Even before Vorster resigned as prime minister in October 1978, "the second most powerful man in the country," General van den Bergh, stepped down in a barrage of criticism. During his tenure he had built BOSS into a formidable and feared institution. In retrospect, however, it was a house of cards. He had also become the confidant of the prime minister and had provided the impetus for a vigorous South African policy of detente in the region and throughout Africa. That, too, was stillborn. And van den Bergh was central to many schemes of the Department of Information, an edifice that collapsed on top of him and his patron. Finally, he had challenged openly the man who was to become the next prime minister, on matters of intelligence, strategy, and foreign policy.

Meanwhile, however, MIS (it was renamed the Military Intelligence Section in 1971) saw its star rise as Botha took command and pulled along with him various security agencies. A major review of the intelligence service, undertaken by a former director of MIS, concluded that MIS should be central to the total enterprise. Botha consolidated his control of the intelligence services by naming Kobie Coetsee as deputy minister of defence and of national security and by asking Coetsee to study the roles of the security forces. Without van den Bergh and Vorster to shield it, DONS lost its special status in the intelligence hierarchy. Van den Bergh's tenure as secretary for state security had not erased rivalry between intelligence branches. MIS had been overshadowed but not overwhelmed. The Security Police resisted BOSS domination, too.

To this day, competition is intense. DONS, renamed again the NIS, with a new leader, Dr. Lukas Daniel "Niel" Barnard, has an unclear mission. It has been reestablished as an intelligence evaluation center, a think tank rather than a gatherer of intelligence. But operatives accustomed to active policy roles seldom are content as passive analysts. MIS seems to have taken responsibility for covert external intelligence gathering. The Security Branch focusses on domestic intelligence. Responsibility for covert operations or "dirty tricks," to apply the American argot, is more difficult to determine. Top-level policy advice seems to come from a number of SADF offices and officers. The Security Police, however, have not been entirely bypassed, indeed their chief officer was recently promoted to commissioner of police, thereby giving him a direct presence in the State Security Council. NIS has been downgraded in importance in relation to the other intelligence agencies. No manifest logical division of intelligence labor exists, and that leaves the field open for competition and claims to responsibility and authority. Each agency tries to enlarge its own jurisdiction at the expense of rivals.

Now it appears (and it must be emphasized that this is conjecture) that MIS is on top, with NIS on the bottom. All intelligence agencies operate with great secrecy. Both MIS and NIS, however, have been tarnished by their alleged involvement in the unsuccessful Seychelles coup attempt, or conversely, by their inability to see it being planned, when South Africans and even some of their ex-agents were involved.[12] In either case, the operation does not reflect well on MIS and NIS, and, as a result, the Security Branch by default seems to have emerged relatively unscathed from the Seychelles debacle.

A third segment of the security establishment is that element of the intellectual community that serves parts of the security establishment on an ad hoc contractual basis. There are, for example, various centers of strategic studies. Perhaps the most active and influential is the Institute for Strategic Studies at the University of Pretoria. In the past it had been provided funds by the Department of Information. Another center at the Rand Afrikaans University is headed by a former director of Military Intelligence, and the center at UNISA is led by a former Citizens Force officer.[13] Faculty and researchers from these centers participate in discussion groups, planning sessions, and advisory bodies, and they regularly address various classes in diverse military and police training programs. They also do contract work for the SADF and other security bodies, and some have been included in delegations to foreign governments and institutions.

In addition, private independent firms are engaged increasingly in research and policy advice on security and strategy. Among these groups would be the Terrorism Research Centre in Cape Town, Ron Reid-Daly's team of security technicians in Johannesburg, and other private firms advising private industry and parastatal corporations on improving their security to comply with the National Key Points Act of 1980 and to protect their executives from terrorist attacks and kidnappings. Many firms are anxious to cash in on the provisions of the National Key Point Act and the growing concern of executives about corporate and personal security. Pages of the trade journals are filled with their advertisements, and during the initial implementation phases of the Act, business is growing.[14] In some instances, however, there is question as to how independent such groups are. Gordon Winter, hardly reliable in the past, maintains that Michael Morris of the Terrorism Research Centre worked for RI and BOSS until 1973 and that the TRC was (and may still be) a front organization for BOSS and its successors.[15]

Individual academics interested in strategy and security are also drawn into the policy process, usually remotely, occasionally directly. They testify before governmental commissions, engage in contracted research, help train security and government personnel, write for government and private publications (on behalf of government's line), and in general make their advice and reputations available to the authorities. On a more technical level individual university faculty members and departments, especially at the Afrikaner universities, have undertaken defense-related research.[16] Particularly through the Council for Scientific and Industrial Research (CSIR) and the Human Sciences Research Council (HSRC), students and academic staff investigate subjects of value to the SADF and Armscor. Some are funded by grants presumably emanating from the Department of Defence.

The armaments and related industries are part of the security establishment, too. Frankel sees this as a "lower-order version" of C. Wright Mills's concept of the "military-industrial complex." The analogy is not inappropriate.[17] Most prominent are the parastatal corporations directly a part of the security enterprise. The Armaments Development and Manufacturing Corporation of South Africa (Armscor) exists solely to improve the material defense capabilities of the state.[18] Like the SADF itself, Armscor comes directly under the authority of the Minister of Defence. It is one of the biggest industrial undertakings in South Africa, with assets greater than R1,617 million, 650 percent greater than its holdings of R200 million in 1974. This places Armscor among South Africa's top twenty companies. Armscor directly employs around 23,000 and provides work for over 100,000 people through its nine subsidiaries and its 3,000 private subcontractors.[19]

The upshot of this growth is that Armscor is now the world's tenth largest arms manufacturer. Whereas twelve years ago about 70 percent of the defense budget went to material imports, today military imports represent only about 15 percent of the defense budget. Imports can be expected to increase as operational expenses are reduced and the need to replace obsolescent material increases. Armscor was created partially in response to a UN arms embargo. Today it is in a position to export weapons. For political reasons it is not easy to find customers, but export promotions are ambitious.

Through Armscor subsidiaries and by means of managerial advisory groups, Armscor has deep links with private sector firms and research companies. Indeed, it is Armscor's stated policy to make "maximum utilization of the private sector." Around 70 percent of Armscor's production is contracted out to the private sector. This partnership with private enterprise dates from the time when P. W. Botha was minister of defense. He gathered around him advisors from private firms, and that closeness persists today. Armscor tenders touch practically every sector of modern industry. Some of the country's top industrialists and managers serve on various group boards. Barlow Rand seconded John Maree to Armscor for three years, and he reorganized the corporation to make better use of the private sector. The main Armscor board is appointed by the state president and is responsible to the minister of defense. It includes the chief of the SADF and the director-general of finance. The rest are mostly from private finance, manufacturing, and commerce. Armscor does not make public the names of its directors so as not to harm their foreign business interests. But the concept of private-state cooperation for state security is well advanced by Armscor and is regarded by some planners as a model to be applied elsewhere.

Other parastatal corporations, Sasol (oil) and Iscor (steel) for examples, also have defense and security links through planning bodies and through sales to security forces and other state organs. CSIR, among other state-run bodies, is totally tied to defense research, especially in the technologies of communications, rocketry, radar, and armor. Moreover, the terms of legislation such as the Atomic Energy Act as amended in 1979, the

National Supplies Procurement Act of 1970 as amended in 1979, and the Petroleum Products Amendment Act of 1979, require that firms not disclose certain data about their operations. These laws, for their part, commit the private sector to the total national strategy.

Not only Armscor but other parastatal corporations are also the conduits through which the private business sectors have been engaged in the security of the state. The Carlton (November 1979) and Good Hope (November 1981) meetings at which the prime minister sought to explain and discuss with private business leaders his plans, to elicit from them ideas and reactions to his government's proposals, and to involve them more closely with his future visions serve, among other things, to punctuate a linkage that P. W. Botha seeks to develop.[20] Government fears a "Marxist onslaught." To combat Marxism, who better but capitalist proponents?

As in all political regimes that purport to be representative, various social groups seek to expand their access and role in government. In South Africa the corporate world likewise seeks to enlarge its voice in public decision-making bodies at the same time that it wishes to maintain its political and especially its partisan distance. The idea of total national strategy, propounded by an individual (P. W. Botha) and an institution identified with managerial modernization (the SADF), enhances the private sector's confidence in government.[21] Business leaders, after all, admire managerial efficiency. The thirteen-man Defence Advisory Council, whose membership is an elite of big business, has been one possible medium for this involvement of the private sector in the total strategy, but it has not proven altogether satisfactory from government's standpoint. It has been relatively inactive since its formation. When members' terms expired on 31 March 1982, they were not reappointed. Defence Minister Malan explained that the council had become superfluous, especially with the restructuring of the Defence Manpower Liaison Committee. The DMLC has served to help the Defence Department develop guidelines for the Defence Amendment Act. It is almost exclusively concerned with manpower questions. Most large employment organizations are involved in the committee as is the Department of Manpower Utilization and Development. As such it was not designed to replace the Defence Advisory Council, whose mandate was more in the line of finance, weapons and material development and manufacture, and the larger political-economic matters related to commerce and industry. Consequently some people speculate that in fact the council has not been dissolved.[22] There is also a Defence Research and Development Council to coordinate R and D in defense fields with private sector firms and with scientific personnel working for government, the universities, and industries.

Lest anyone by misled into thinking that South Africa is entirely self-sufficient in armaments, South Africa has regularly been forced to enter the arms market abroad to purchase selected material. But the international arms sanctions against South Africa have forced Pretoria to develop elaborate machinery for eluding embargoes.[23] In 1984 part of this clandestine corporate network came to light in the United Kingdom with the arrest in London of four South African business agents. They were accused of contravening Britain's arms control regulations by illegally exporting arms-related goods worth up to R2 million.[24] Certainly the world had been forewarned. "So if what we are fighting for is worth it, then we will fight dirty if need be," stated Armscor executive general manager, Fred Bell.[25] South Africa needed the foreign technology for its own weapons development, and she would acquire it at all costs. The *Guardian* of London was to disclose the complex and intricate corporate structures established by Pretoria and ultimately linked to Safmarine, a government-owned parastatal shipping line.[26] Devious steps were taken to mask this linkage, and a number of South African and British private firms contributed to the ruse. Such arrangements were similar to those fashioned to evade sanctions against Rhodesia. Many of the same firms and personalities were involved as well. How many hidden firms are already in place in other countries to expedite the acquisition of armaments and military technology?

It may be a bit overdrawn to speak of a military-industrial complex in Millsian terms. The American model is so deeply entrenched and so much larger and more elaborate. But the "partnership," as Deon Geldenhuys calls it, is genuine and mutually supportive. Many firms now have vested interests in seeing their links with the Defence Department flourish, and in the process they may help to influence government decisions on armament questions as government has been able to influence the firms. On logistical matters the interaction is undeniable. Whether it extends to larger strategic questions is doubtful. If Armscor should begin to develop an export capacity, then business input into foreign policy decisions might expand, as it has in, for example, the United States.

(5)   A fifth component of the security establishment is the South African Police (SAP). There is no need to detail the role of SAP in maintaining state security.[27] Perhaps less public are the paramilitary formations that patrol the borders, that are used to put down internal unrest, and that have been deployed in the operational areas of Namibia and Rhodesia. In all these activities and others, there is a high level of interaction and cooperation between SAP and SADF.[28] Although SADF has sought to avoid the stigma of repressing the civil population, in fact the SADF has widened its range of domestic deployment and in the process finds its popular image more closely identified with the apartheid policies of the government and hence of the National Party.

VI. THE STATE SECURITY COUNCIL

(6)

Many of these organizations and their functions are brought together in the workings of the sixth element of the security establishment—the State Security Council (SSC). The SSC is the central organization through which security policy is determined and its implementation is coordinated. In the secrecy that attends this organization and in its composition involving the very highest leaders of the ruling party, it is not unlike the National Defense Council of the Soviet Union. But the SSC goes beyond its Soviet counterpart. The latter is concerned chiefly with Soviet military policy.[29] The SSC perceives its assignment broadly, with military matters just one, albeit the most important, facet of state security. The SSC, in addition, serves as the most important cabinet committee in a variety of other issue areas, including foreign policy, many economic decisions, some issues of justice, and even key apartheid and constitutional questions.

Technically the SSC is but one among four pivotal cabinet committees. In fact, it is primus inter pares. In the first place, it is chaired by the prime minister (now state president) himself. Secondly, it is the only cabinet committee established by law with a fixed membership, and although this in itself was not enough to make the SSC so pivotal in the Vorster regime, it adds to the impact of the body when coupled with other factors. Thirdly, it is apparent that the SSC has a range of interests wider than other cabinet committees. The SSC's statutory mandate is to advise government on the formulation and implementation "of national policy and strategy in relation to the security of the Republic." Its members subscribe to and propagate the necessity of a "total national strategy" to combat a "total onslaught" aimed at South Africa. The SSC has an inflated sense of its responsibility.

Each of the other three cabinet committees have only five full-time employees in their secretariats. They must rely on the cabinet secretariat for larger assignments. The SSC has around fifty. Thus, the SSC has a complex of supporting agencies and committees more extensive and complete than any other cabinet committee. Seen from this vantage, practically no facet of state policy can be excluded from some aspect of security affairs. In addition, the meetings of the three other cabinet committees are open to ministers who are not formally members. In the SSC, non-primary members may not attend unless explicitly invited to the meeting. In short, an air of importance and exclusivity is attached to SSC meetings that does not apply to other cabinet committees.

In September 1983 the government sought to deflect such assertions about the SSC in a most unusual press conference. In direct response to academic and popular publications that claimed that the SSC, or more generally the security establishment, was effectively shaping state policy in a variety of nonstrategic fields as well as in strategy,[30] the prime minister called a conference chaired by Deputy Minister of Information Barend du Plessis. At this conference the SSC's secretary, Lt. Gen. A. J. van Deventer, and Dr. J. P. "Jannie" Roux, secretary of the Department of the Prime Minister, addressed the press.[31]

Van Deventer, generally a nonpublic figure who seldom if ever meets the press, did most of the talking. He argued, in effect, that the SSC was just one among four cabinet committees—it had no executive authority, and all its recommendations were subject to final cabinet approval. To be sure, the SSC has chiefly advisory functions by law. So does the Politburo of the CPSU, but who would deny its power? Effective decision-making authority in South Africa resides in the SSC if one looks at the actual political relationships instead of at the organizational charts and the formal institutional legalisms.

Part of van Deventer's message was an effort to show that there is nothing unusual in the present arrangements—that in South Africa in the past, prime ministers have been advised on security matters (which is true) and that in other countries (he used the example of the U.S. National Security Council) state security is an important policy area (which is also true). What he failed explicitly to state was how central security has become in South Africa. This, too, may not be unusual, but it is a change in emphasis for South African governments. Yet, in the process of denying inordinate importance for the SSC, a picture was painted of a decision-making system very much centered around an executive government, the hub of which is the SSC. Van Deventer sought to justify this concentration of power in terms of a full-fledged offensive aimed at South Africa and directed from Moscow.

The reality that did emerge—and there were new disclosures and insights into the inner workings of the executive—tended to confirm the strong SSC military-centric thesis that the press conference was intended to dispell. The disclosures also confirmed the contention that virtually all foreign and domestic matters are fit subjects for the SSC. For example, at the SSC meeting prior to the press conference, van Deventer said that "as many as 10 Ministers attended." Because of the massive threat against South Africa, the SSC has become the needed "coordinating forum" in respect to national security.

Although the full membership of the SSC has never been publicly disclosed, it includes at least the following: the prime minister (now the state president) and the ministers of foreign affairs, defense, police (now law and order), justice, and the most senior cabinet minister.[32] In SSC nomenclature, the standing members are known as "primary members." At present, "primary members" include some others who regularly attend but are not so named in the law. This includes the ministers of finance,

So, in held policy the opp exists for superb co-ord & extreme conflict over policy among the urb. commu.

cooperation and development, and constitutional development and planning. Each are ministers who chair the other three cabinet committees and thus are coopted members.

The SSC also includes the top-ranking civil servants/career professionals in each of those key departments. Thus the directors-general of foreign affairs and justice, the director-general of the Department of the State President, the chief of the SADF, the commissioner of police, and the head of the NIS participate. A number of important people *not* directly responsible to parliament participate in the decisional process at the highest levels. Others in government and in private life may be invited to attend individual meetings, depending on the subject at hand and the nature of the expertise they might be expected to provide. If, for example, weapons development is on the agenda, the director of Armscor may be asked to attend. If the topic is regional economic growth or transport planning as it impacts on foreign policy the general manager of the S.A. Transport Services may be coopted. The SSC is a body composed of political heavyweights supplemented by the highest-ranking political and governmental experts in security and strategy. When they recommend policy, the cabinet is not likely to deny them. It is the prestige and influence associated with the individuals and their offices that assure that the SSC continues at the hub of governmental decision making in so many areas of state policy.

Granted, the official organizational chart of the cabinet committee system depicts clearly the formal relationships at the center (see fig. 1). What it fails to reveal are the informal links and relative weights of the committees accruing from the occupants of the various roles. Nor does it indicate directions of authority and control. A great deal may be inferred from the dotted line between the SSC and the prime minister. What is unpictured, notably the secretariat of the SSC and the Joint Management Centres, might add to a better understanding.

The operation of the SSC and the entire security management system has evolved markedly since the 1972 legislation creating the SSC went into force. Originally the SSC's function was to advise the government with regard to the formulation of national policy and strategy and to determine intelligence priorities. It was, at that time, just one of twenty different cabinet committees. Cabinet committees under Vorster operated in an ad hoc fashion. If a problem arose, a committee was called to deal with it. Thus the SSC met sporadically, as did other cabinet committees. There was little coordination of committee actions.[33] The SSC was clearly subordinate to the cabinet, politically as well as legally.

P. W. Botha as minister of defense engineered a transformation in the SSC and later, as prime minister, in the entire decisional and executive

Fig. 1. Structure of the Cabinet Committee System
as outlined by Dr. J. P. Roux, Secretary of the Department of
the Prime Minister at a press conference, September, 1983.

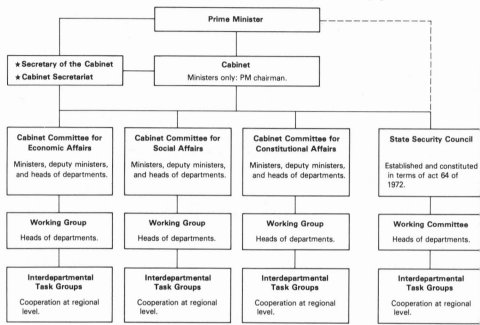

Source: "State Security Council: Not Sinister!" *Paratus*, vol. 34, no. 11 (November, 1983),
p. 11.

apparatus. These changes were largely structural and administrative.
Committees would operate on a regular basis with clearly demarcated
briefs. A rational flow of paper would enable the prime minister to receive
information and instruct governmental and bureaucratic personnel in
order to enable government policy to be carried out. The object was to
end guesswork and ad hoc-ery.

   In 1973 an investigation was held into the shortcomings of the state
machinery for security. A Report on the National Security Situation was
completed by the Public Service Commission in September 1975, and
its most important provisions were eventually implemented, especially
in the area of administration and coordination of policy. The report recommended, inter alia, the establishment of an active security management
system to link national, interdepartmental, departmental, and subde-
partmental levels of operation. A full-time national security staff would
be needed. For regional and local levels, area and regional committees
were created to facilitate coordination. Fifteen functional areas of concern
were identified within the security field, and committees were established

for each. The wide-ranging areas covered virtually every facet of state policy, from culture to civil defense, from economy to manpower.

South Africa's involvement in the Angolan civil war only confirmed Botha's desire to reorganize. According to General Malan, the Angolan war "focussed the attention on the urgent necessity for the State Security Council to play a much fuller role in the national security of the Republic than hitherto."[34] An interdepartmental committee on the issue of national strategy formulation and organization recommended the creation of a working committee of the SSC. This was to consist of senior represen- tatives from each department permanently a part of the SSC. Others could be coopted. In addition a permanent secretariat of the SSC was recommended to be headed by the secretary of the SSC. He would also serve as chairman of the working committee. Lt. Gen. van Deventer thereby provided the continuity at the core of almost all security planning activity. The secretariat was instituted in 1979.

The working committee and behind it the secretariat are poised to shape agendas, develop position papers, formulate alternatives, take and circulate minutes, and, once the SSC and the cabinet have acted, to see to it that each operational department and bureau knows what is expected of it, that decisions are circulated to relevant officials, and that cooperation and coordination are assured.

The secretariat consists of four branches. *Strategy* is responsible for formulating strategy and plans and for coordinating the monitoring of policy implementation among executive departments. *National Intelli- gence Interpretation* evaluates intelligence coming in from SAP, SADF, NIS, and DFAI. This in turn is reported to the SSC and the cabinet for planning purposes. *Stategic Communication* provides advice and coor- dination to departments regarding their own propaganda needs, and *Administration* provides the organizational-administrative cement to the operation. All in all there are around fifty to sixty employees in the secretariat (not counting its subordinate working committees). Perhaps stung by charges that the SADF dominated the SSC, in early 1984 Prime Minister Botha claimed in parliament that 56 percent of SSC secretariat staff are supplied by the NIS, 11 percent each from the security police and the department of foreign affairs, 5 percent from the railway police, and 1 percent from the prisons service. This leaves just 16 percent from the SADF. "Where is the domination?" he asked rhetorically.[35] The administrative linkage of the SSC's secretariat to the NIS contributes to the latter's numerical preponderance, as does the SSC's concentration on intelligence evaluation. The formalization and enlargement of the sec- retariat of the SSC led to a proportionate decline in the seconded SADF personnel.

Also created were organizations responsible for national security at local and regional levels to coordinate the activities of these departments and other organizations. These are known as Joint Management Centres (officially known in Afrikaans as GBSs, for *Gesamentlike Bestuurssentrums*). Nine GBSs serve geographical areas that coincide with the area commands of the SADF. A tenth is for Walvis Bay, and four more are responsible for designated southern African countries (e.g., Namibia). Most are composed of senior officials (especially SADF officers).

When P. W. Botha became prime minister the process of change in the Security Management System was speeded up and extended. To begin with, Botha reduced the number of cabinet committees from twenty to five permanent committees. He introduced regular (fortnightly) meetings and rearranged their timing so that SSC meetings now precede cabinet meetings. The appearance of the SSC presenting the cabinet with completed decisions has been noted.[36] In addition, the SSC holds meetings when parliament is in recess and when the cabinet is inactive. The SSC again would seem to provide executive continuity, particularly on matters of security, even though in formal terms the cabinet is paramount.

Although the institutional responsibilities of the members of the SSC are largely unchanged in the past ten years, the perceptions of the individuals occupying these positions have changed. Under Vorster, the SSC was composed of a collection of strong-willed individuals with bases in the Party and keen on maintaining their departmental strengths. In this interlocking directorate they perceived of the cabinet and the Party as their primary base of operations and not the peripatetic SSC. In contrast, under P. W., as the SSC was elevated in prominence, its members began to identify with it as an institution. More key leaders began to see the SSC as an inner cabinet and to regard the full cabinet as less central to the decision-making process. A parallel ironically exists in the politics of the Soviet Union, where there is an interlocking directorate at the top. Powerful individuals hold positions in both government and in the politburo of the Communist party. But without question they regard their standing in the politburo as more important than their position in the Council of Ministers—one is clearly the decisional locus, the other is a legalistic rubber-stamp and policy-coordinating body. Party prevails over government. Those who misjudge the situation, as did Georgi Malenkov, find their political careers side-tracked or shortened. Although it is clearly premature to regard this as pattern that applies in South Africa—after all, it involves just one government, that of P. W. Botha—the parallel cannot be ignored, since it does represent a possible formula for imposing marginal (though symbolically significant) reforms on a constituency that may balk or resist.

To be sure, not all top cabinet officers identify with the SSC in preference to a political base in their department or in the provincial or central Party apparatus. Most would prefer to retain all their political options in an as yet fluid situation. South African politicians are too individualistic, their styles too practical to conform to some analytical model developed to explain political patterns elsewhere. Nevertheless, in the aggregate this tendency to identify with the institution of the SSC should not be ignored.

By the nature of governmental and administrative reorganization, the SSC has the advantage of being the principal originating and coordinating organ for the total national strategy, "the focal point of all national decision-making and governmental power," as one analyst, perhaps with a bit of overstatement, put it.[37] The SSC's agenda has widened as awareness of "total onslaught" has grown and as commitment to "total national strategy," broadly constructed, has taken root. It is an atmosphere in which, if you don't believe in "total onslaught" you, ipso facto, contribute unwittingly to that onslaught. It is inherently a polarizing outlook, and it applies even with the downplay of the term and the diplomatic openings to Marxist neighboring states.

Other changes in executive organization, by default, gave the SSC and its ancillary secretariat further advantages. The number of government departments was reduced from thirty-nine (in April 1980) to twenty-two. Since the new constitution came into force this was further reduced to eighteen for "general affairs," plus fifteen more in the three ministers' councils that deal with "own affairs." The Department of the State President has been expanded and organized to parallel the structure of cabinet committees. A cabinet secretariat has been established. There are agendas for cabinet meetings and minutes are kept. The secretary-general of the Department of the State President manages cabinet business, in preparation for its weekly meetings and in execution of its decisions. He and Lt. Gen. van Deventer are crucial to the new, rationalized order. In 1982, the security planning section of the prime minister's office was moved administratively out of the prime minister's office into the NIS. But rather than this representing an enhancement of NIS power[38] it is more likely a convenience move to enable Lt. Gen. van Deventer to report directly to the SSC and the prime minister (the dotted line in fig. 1) without having to work through the then director general of the Office of the Prime Minister, Dr. J. E. du Plessis. In other words, the secretariat is now even more independent. The decision-making process has been centralized, and placed firmly at the hub of the process is the state president, the SSC, and its secretariat.

To add to the importance of the military establishment, SADF officers are prominent in all high-level interdepartmental committees of the SSC. DFAI is represented on only four of those interdepartmental committees. SADF has also had a direct input into diverse governmental commissions and investigatory bodies through petition, testimony, submission of evidence, and deputation. Often representatives of SSC (not always military persons) sit on these panels. Just a few examples should suffice to demonstrate that they cast a wide net. Since 1982 the secretariat of the SSC has had a spokesman on KEOSSA (the Afrikaans acronym for the Committee for Economic and Development Co-operation in Southern Africa) even though the enterprise is largely associated with agricultural development, finance, and foreign affairs in the "national states." Similarly, SADF has limited representation (General Malan himself) on the Central Consolidation Committee of the Commission for Co-operation and Development (the van der Walt Commission) and is actively involved in its Defence and Strategy subcommittee. This commission, formed in 1979, is to formulate proposals for the consolidation of the homelands territorial parcels. The SADF has seconded and allotted national servicemen to work in various governmental departments, in some cases in uniform. Often they draw their pay from the SADF. The SADF has supplied researchers to the Human Science Research Council to study press reporting for its report to the Steyn Commission of Inquiry into the Mass Media. In another instance, SADF reportedly had a direct role in drafting the clauses dealing with curfews in the Orderly Movement and Settlement of Black Persons Bill.[39]

The SADF is torn between its enlightened or reformist mode, which is characterized by the philosophy of "winning hearts and minds," and a more repressive "peace, law, and order" outlook. Although there is nothing inherently pernicious about these SADF links to governmental bodies, they do illustrate the ubiquity of such security ties and their potential for influence. They also exemplify a salient departure from past practice. The national security management system represents the triumph of the SADF in its ongoing struggle with BOSS/DONS/NIS, SAP, and of course the DFAI. How long it can sustain that ascendency is probably a function of the political staying power of P. W. Botha himself, especially now that he occupies the new position of executive state president.

As P. W. Botha devises these organizational changes one cannot help but think that there is, indeed, purpose and design to his steps. Agreed that there is a good deal of rationalization in these measures and that efficiency has its own rewards. But underlying these changes is a widely held belief that the prime minister was clearing the decks for action—not merely for fighting a war with violent opponents of the regime, but for fashioning significant political changes in order to outflank those opponents. Ironically, the nature and extent of these changes depend as much on those not at all represented on these bodies or in the latest constitutional schemes—black South Africans, and to a lesser extent on those Coloured and Indian people and their leaders who are inclined to resist being drafted into an order that still does not give them fully equal status and that excludes, and is not even envisioned to include, their black brothers.

In the remainder of this book I shall examine some issues in which the hand of the security establishment is marking the outcome. These concerns do not represent a complete picture of defense involvement in matters not entirely defensive or strategic in nature. Rather they are used to illustrate some of the broad observations and generalizations noted in the preceding chapters and to suggest an evolving pattern for future political alignments and contests.

CHAPTER IV

The Militarization
of White Society

An outsider who returns to South Africa periodically can discern a rising
visibility of things martial creeping into what had theretofore been regarded as exclusively civilian affairs. Few in South Africa would care to
acknowledge this trend, especially in that it unfolds imperceptively. This
is not to say that South Africa is fully mobilized or even extensively
mobilized. One student has referred to a "war psychosis," but that is
extravagant. Nor should we fear, as did one Nationalist member of parliament, that the "peace initiatives" of early 1984 had been so successful
that South Africans must "guard against lapsing into a psychosis of peace."[1]
Rather South Africans face a growing sense of insecurity and a commitment to resist significant power shifts, if need be, by force. It is a changing
atmosphere that can be appreciated, just as one can observe tangible
changes in preparations for the coming confrontation. In this study militarization is seen as a process rather than as an accomplished fact. Obviously these tendencies predate P. W. Botha's ascension to power. As
this process has evolved there has been a conscious creation of a social
atmosphere that makes military service appear attractive, military responses to policy issues sensible, and greater military strength and expenditure necessary and acceptable—a mood which generally prepares
the population for sacrifice under circumstances perceived to be isolation,
siege, or even war.

I. THE FORMAL
EDUCATIONAL INSTITUTIONS

It is widely agreed that school is a major instrument of socialization.
Schools are the vehicle by which a modern society transmits its most
important values to young people and by which society identifies and
trains its next generation of leaders. In South Africa the socialization
process has recently taken on an expanded, if not entirely new, dimension.
This entails the deepening militarization of the white educational process.[2]

This involves a changing relation between the SADF and the departments of National Education, Education and Training, and Internal Affairs. The SADF plays a greater role these days in shaping some facets of educational policy.

Cadet detachments have been set up in white boys' secondary schools, and, since 1976, the cadet program has been directly under the control of the SADF.[3] Some 170,000 boys in 1983 were provided paramilitary drill and training, and were psychologically prepared for national service. This is compulsory for white boys in all government schools, and compulsory cadet training is planned for white girls. Cadets are encouraged to enlist in the Permanent Force (PF) upon graduation. In some schools cadet detachments have been directly affiliated with PF and Citizen Force regiments. Officers and NCOs regularly visit schools (including schools for Coloured and Indian children) in connection with youth preparedness, career guidance, information with respect to national service, the selection of boys for special schools for national service, and activities regarding the training of school cadets.[4]

Some students attend two-week camps during holidays. There, school teachers who also double as military officers subject them to a routine of activities resembling what they can expect in the SADF.[5] Even before senior high school, youngsters in the Transvaal are urged to attend voluntary week-long veld schools ostensibly for the purpose of environmental education and outdoor survival techniques. Also included is a heady dose of political and (some would say) partisan indoctrination and paramilitary discipline.[6] The Transvaal Education Department controls these veld schools and expounds a right-wing ideology not to the liking entirely of even P. W. Botha and General Malan. *Verkrampte* (inflexible and racist) instructors propound a total onslaught message, yet they seem to be out of step with the SADF's reformist "multi-racialism."[7] In the Cape Province there is a scaled-down form of veld school without the military emphasis. Elementary school students and even nursery school children (ages three to six) are taken for visits to military installations.[8]

II. PRESS RELATIONS

In addition, the news and entertainment media, particularly state-owned and operated radio and television networks and the Publications Control Board, contribute to a largely one-sided milieu that serves to promote and glorify but not romanticize military service. In mid-1977 SADF established its own public relations branch on a full-time basis. Professional journalists were brought into the service, and the volume and quality of press releases and liaison improved.[9] The SADF took a firm grip on its own extensive list of publications to sharpen the ideological message.[10]

Self-censorship in response to tightened secrecy and imposed journalistic restraints in the form of a battery of prior censorship laws and postpublication penalties account for a situation in which the security establishment is seldom mentioned except in favorable terms. Section 118 of the Defence Act, for example, prohibits statements about military activity that are "calculated to prejudice or embarrass the government or to alarm or depress members of the public." All reports of all SADF military movements and of police counterinsurgency actions or even of acts of sabotage have to be passed by military or police authorities before publication. The important thing is not what is said in the press, but what is not said. Laws that censor or limit reportage on security matters fuel speculation in place of hard fact. This policy itself contributes to some of the exaggerations among outsiders and regime opponents. Public confidence suffers. Greater candor might, within its own constituency, serve government well.[11] A case in point is the 1982 situation involving reporters who sought to dig deeply into MIS and other SADF involvement in the Seychelles coup attempt and cover-up. What David S. Broder has called the Granada rule applies here: "no reporters are allowed on the scene until the mess has been cleared up."[12]

In other places there appear to be limits as to how willing the media are to be manipulated. At one point, SABC production personnel (government employees) refused to be associated with a saber-rattling and propagandistic "documentary" on the SADF. A private company had to be hired to film the show.[13] The press can be pressured, directly and indirectly. For example, the SADF made submissions to the Steyn Commission of Inquiry into the Mass Media, and SADF seconded researchers to the HSRC to study press coverage of the security forces for that commission.

Part of the positive image of the SADF then is attributable to outright intimidation and legislative control, part to self-restraint, part to conscious public relations and, of course, part grows out of a genuine admiration for the effectiveness and professionalism of the SADF. The press liaison and public relations sections of the SADF have been steadily enlarged and professionalized over the years. Efforts have been made to engage large segments of the civilian population in support programs to assist national servicemen before, during, and after their service, and to help SADF members adjust to their lives and sacrifices.

III. CIVIC ACTION

The Civic Action arms of the SADF also contribute to an overall affirmation of military virtue. The government and the SADF often refer to a "winning hearts and minds" (WHAM) philosophy with regard to the blacks.[14] Here the emphasis is on painting the SADF in a favorable light in order to deny insurgents the psychological advantage of being more popular than the defense forces. The rationale is that, if the SADF provides the people with needed services and assistance, perhaps the people will support the insurgents less and be positively helpful to the SADF and the South African authorities. Noncombat activities thus strive for a dual purpose, to win allies among the people and to supply the combat arm with intelligence that can be gleaned only from the local population. As part of the practical and propaganda strategies undergirding WHAM, the SADF in January 1978 established a subsection of *Burgersake* or Civic Action. Before 1978 similar assignments were performed by an organization operating in Namibia which, since 1974, had been a part of the South African Army. In time the activities of the Civic Action program were expanded, and the functions were divided. The Civic Action subsection concentrated on policy and coordination and the executive functions remained with the branches of the service, mainly the army. *Burgersake* was headed by the Chief of Staff: Operations, Major General Phil Pretorius, a former commander of the Transkeian Defence Force and secretary of defense to the Transkeian government. Pretorius is also trained in psychological warfare. After a March 1980 partisan political flap (see the following section), the directorate of Civic Action was abolished, although the Civic Action program itself has been continued.

National servicemen in Civic Action perform mostly as teachers, agricultural specialists, medical doctors, engineers, and administrators. They work throughout South Africa and Namibia, in the homelands and in various other black venues. Their aim is to improve relations with the black residents, and in the process to gather intelligence that may be politically and militarily useful to the regime. Some have worked in schools in urban townships, in which case the propaganda message may become heavy and may damage intergroup relations. Most national servicemen in these situations serve in full uniform, including holstered revolvers. Complaints regarding such activities have taken various forms, although in some instances Coloured and black principals have commended the dedication and teaching skills of the national servicemen. On at least one occasion, however, the SADF teachers distributed copies of a SADF magazine, the *Warrior*, in which it was claimed that there is freedom in South Africa and that the true leaders of the black people are not "convicts" such as Nelson Mandela but Community Council officers such as David Thebehali. In protest against this "gun toting battalion" some students boycotted classes.[15] When the idea of national service teachers was first suggested for Soweto, prominent black spokespersons objected.[16]

When Civic Action was first conceived, it was regarded as very much the professional, modern way to combat civil unrest. The psychological weapon was to be one of the most powerful arrows in the SADF quiver. General Malan had stressed time and again the need to gain the "trust and faith" of blacks in order to foil insurgency.[17] On paper Civic Action makes sense. Some departments of state have difficulty persuading young, urbanized civil servants to accept assignments in rural areas. Under the guise of military discipline such services can be supplied. The idea of the social welfare services being provided by compulsory service formations also has been advanced by the PFP. MP Ray Swart, for example, has suggested that a multiracial, volunteer "peace corps"-type organization be established and linked to the SADF (perhaps as a form of alternative service).[18]

But psychological operations and Civic Action convince few blacks, even in those instances in which Civic Action supplies much-needed and much-appreciated social services. The problems are not so much the personality or methods of those leading Civic Action but the fact that the program is rightly perceived to be, in essence, a part of the government's "total national strategy" designed at heart to perpetuate white control and privilege. Civic Action involves the deployment of national service-men doing their obligatory military service. Although they may be fur-nishing social services, their activities have a basic security purpose. Defence Headquarters and strategic planners clearly see Civic Action in its overall strategic and security contexts. In short, although Civic Action may have positive ramifications for the lives of some black South Africans in terms of the social services it provides, it is principally an instrument of control. In the minds of the inhabitants of Namibia, for instance, noncoercive activities of the SADF and South West Africa Territorial Force (SWATF) cannot be separated from the notoriously violent and cruel actions of COIN units. Both are part of the same regime and hence work to the same ends in the popular mind. Moreover, Civic Action involves virtually no black input in deciding which programs to undertake or how to manage them in the interests of the subject peoples. Civic Action represents another way in which the SADF has insinuated itself where the political and social overtones amount to the militarization of South African society.

IV. INVOLVEMENT OF THE SADF IN PARTISAN POLITICS

It is not easy for an armed force to avoid charges that its members or its corporate policy preferences favor one party or another in a multi-party state. In the South African context, where the history of the Defence

Force is intertwined with the struggle for political ascendance between English-speakers and Afrikaners, absolute neutrality has been nearly impossible to achieve. Moreover, all South Africans must acknowledge that the SADF is first and foremost an instrument of white rule. It is hardly a homogenous social unit and by no means a faithful reflection of the society it "defends." The SADF has tended to be identified closely with the policies of the dominant wing of the ruling party. It is also a major contributor to the instigation of those policies.

Thus when, as occasionally happens, the SADF or segments of it are accused of supporting the National Party or particular partisan policies, it is surprising how indignant politicians can become. Take an instructive 1980 case, one that evaporated almost as mercurially as it materialized.

On 23 March 1980 the *Sunday Times* published a story about an SADF document headed "Psychological Action Plan: Defence Budget Debate" and dated 12 February 1980. That document detailed secret steps to manipulate the news media in order to nullify the opposition's criticism of the prime minister. It was signed on behalf of the chief of the SADF, General Malan, by Maj. Gen. Phil Pretorius, at that time director general of Civic Action.

Such a direct effort to manipulate parliamentary affairs and to dabble in partisan politics shocked some observers. SADF personnel are, by law, "nonpolitical." According to a September 1970 SADF order, Permanent Force members may not be members of a political party, may not attend party meetings, demonstrations, or processions in uniform, and are barred from participating in any activity that furthers the interests of candidates for election to public office on a party-political basis. The SADF, after all, has tried to cultivate its professional, nonpartisan image. The Deputy Minister of Defence has said that the policy of his department, since 1966, has been to involve all parties in Parliament in the defense process through parliamentary briefings, visits, and consultations. The SADF is, we have been told repeatedly, a "peoples' army," and an army of all the people of South Africa. Apparently some people matter more than others. Since all legitimate political parties had supported the SADF as an institution in the preceding years, many opposition politicians felt betrayed by this report. The NRP and PFP regularly support larger budgets and generally encourage the *verligtheid* of key SADF leaders. In 1980 SADF apparently had been caught trying to undermine those who criticized the National Party on other issues.

The prime minister, compromised by the report, nonetheless took the offensive, attacking the press and the opposition for their efforts to secure full disclosure and accountability of the matter. P. W. Botha tried to pass the matter off as a minor error of judgment. PFP leader Dr. Frederick Van Zyl Slabbert argued that "if an image is created that the Defence

Force is simply the National Party in uniform, this country will split from top to bottom."[19] Revelation Ntoula of *Voice* tartly jibed Dr. Slabbert: "You see, we Blackies fully perceive the role of the army, but without sounding too nasty to most Black members of the army, it is indeed synonymous with the Nationalist Party."[20]

Critics of the Action Plan focussed their attacks on the SADF's efforts to shape opinion in the House of Assembly. Other features of the plan went uncriticized. By their silence most white politicians implied that SADF dabbling in domestic affairs was acceptable. To seek to channel public opinion and to create a positive image for the SADF is understandable to most politicians. But to turn that propaganda covertly on members of Parliament aroused a howl (among opposition MPs) that the very basis of "democracy" was tottering.[21]

The prime minister rejected the opposition's call for a parliamentary select committee to investigate the SADF's secret Action Plan. Instead, Botha appointed an SADF board of inquiry headed by a former chief of the Defence Force. This in-house investigation, as expected, exonerated the SADF and found no willfulness or negligence by anyone concerned in drawing up, authorizing, handling, or distributing the document. The farthest the report would go was to admit that "serious errors of judgement" had been made. No disciplinary steps were recommended, although shortly before the story broke, the subsection Civic Action was officially terminated, and Maj. Gen. Pretorius was relieved of this command. He was later named chief director of Manpower Development.

Despite this turbulence, within months an SADF pamphlet entitled *The Reason Why* was printed. It, too, propagated the policies of the National Party and attacked the opposition. General Malan repudiated this document as well and promised discipline against those responsible. They had been in violation of an SADF directive requiring all materials affecting party politics to be cleared by the chief of the SADF. Again the internal mechanisms of the Defense Force, at the highest levels, were able to whitewash the embarrassing, yet increasingly to be expected partisan, meddling of the SADF in the country's political life.

Running through the 1984 session of the House of Assembly was a criticism of government and of the SADF for allegedly showing partisan favoritism to the NP in the selection of visitors to the operational area. Both the CP and the PFP raised the issue. One CP member accused government of sending the entire defense study group of the NP to the border on the quiet, and not one member of the three opposition parties accompanied them. Moreover, during the November 1983 referendum campaign, CP speakers were apparently forbidden to talk politics with the soldiers in their bases even though the minister of defense addressed the soldiers. The SADF was, according to the CP, "reduced . . . to the status of a third rate NP organizer."[22]

Related to the referendum, in 1983 a Defence Force magazine, *Contact*, was distributed to Coloured and Indian schools. An article therein suggested mildly that the proposed new constitution should be supported. Considering that both the PFP and the CP opposed the constitutional proposals, that the NP favored them, and that the magazine was distributed at taxpayers' expense, it appears that the SADF was being used for National Party purposes.[23] Government, for its part, denied any secrecy and willful partisan advantage to their policies. But the government's attitude toward opposition parties, especially the CP and PFP, has been negative. The prime minister did not mask his feelings when he stated: "I do not trust the Opposition with security information."[24]

Underlying PFP complaints is a fundamentally skeptical perspective on the social role of the SADF. The CP sees the armed forces as a security shield behind which the status quo can be maintained. The NP shares that view but would presumably permit the forces to facilitate a transition to a new, more defensible status quo. The PFP, by contrast, sees the SADF strictly as an instrument by which South Africa can be defended against external aggression. Meanwhile, the tasks of internal reform must be speeded and extended.[25] If this is the case, it is a wonder that more partisan complaints are not aired. Perhaps their base perspectives are not all that dissimilar.

But let members of the SADF veer from the NP line and government vigorously insists on maintaining the gap between politics and the defense forces. After the formation of the right-wing Afrikaner *Volkswag* in 1984, it was disclosed that several high-ranking commando officers had joined the *Volkswag* branch in Vryburg. The SADF wasted little time in confronting them, despite the fact that they were not members of the Permanent Force and that the *Volkswag* is not strictly a political party (although it is close to the CP). One might ask whether, therefore, the case should be subject to SADF orders against partisan activity.

Within the military itself, the training of troops involves some political indoctrination. This is understandable.[26] But the political line that is transmitted contains a measure of pro-NP publicity, too, and an unflinching advocacy of racial separation. The orientation manual for national servicemen was revised on the protest of opposition MPs, and in another instance the opposition criticized an SADF handbook used for civic guidance programs. The handbooks in question were used to help officers and NCOs prepare lectures to servicemen on "civic guidance"—an integral part of personnel training in which recruits are subjected to lectures and discussions about, inter alia, political ideologies, world affairs, and domestic political and social affairs. The minister of defense, a few days after the protests, released to the press a brief part of the document in question, but defended his department and the handbooks.[27]

Another form of partisan or progovernment intimidation associated with the SADF occurs in the SADF's dealings with local inhabitants in regions where the armed forces are the most direct and, in fact, nearly the only authoritative presence. Obviously the most telling and common form of progovernment action is related to the outright use of armed force. But in situations presumably not calling for the use of coercion, intimidation is subtly and sometimes harshly applied. In Namibia, for example, it has been reported that residents of the Ovambo war zone have been asked under conditions of duress to tell SADF soldiers who they would vote for in an election. It is alleged that each person in a group of nearly a thousand was photographed by a military photographer and their name and answer recorded.[28] In pressure-filled Ovamboland, when the SADF herds together citizens at gunpoint, takes their photograph, and asks "Will you vote for Toivo, the DTA, Shipanga or Kalangula's party?", it takes courage to identify with an antigovernment party. In KwaZulu (the Ingwavuma region), members of the SADF allegedly intimidated Inkatha members and promoted acceptance of the Ingwavuma land deal by asking citizens how they felt about the incorporation of Ingwavuma into Swaziland. The chief of the Army presumably apologized to Chief Buthelezi for the incident.[29]

The Action Plan was a covert scheme to undermine opposition critics in Parliament. The handbooks more openly shaped the political thinking of young servicemen. But in other ways the military participates in internal political manipulation. Within MIS there is purported to be a group that specializes in disinformation. It allegedly has issued fake ANC pamphlets to be circulated locally to "prove" the link between the ANC and foreign-controlled communist movements. The MIS also has been accused of distributing literature to men eligible for national service to make it appear that the literature was from a group supposedly seeking to discourage national service. The pamphlet in question sought to associate this group with enemies of the state. In another instance, a Cape Town labor dispute, the armed forces were charged with forging a Cape Housing Action Committee flyer in order to undercut that group. When the minister of defense was asked if the SADF was involved, he denied knowledge and declined to make a statement.[30] Such suspicions and rumors are commonplace as the "tentacles" of the SADF are seen and imagined "everywhere."

Of course, the Defence Force stoutly denies partisan preferences or pressures. The minister claimed that in 1971 he ruled against a proposal that the General Regulations for the SADF and the Reserve be amended to permit members of the PF to become members of political parties. On his recommendation, the regulations were revised in 1971 to permit PF members nothing more than attendance at public political meetings while dressed in civilian clothes, and the exercise of their voting franchise. Such members may not take part in any activities "for the furtherance of the interests of a political party or of a candidate for partisan election." His stated policy, simply put, is "to keep party politics out of the Defence Force." Moreover, he contends that "political indoctrination is not practised in the South African Defence Force. Our soldiers are, however, motivated against subversion and communism. This is done in an unbiased manner. . . ."[31]

Such assertions are little consolation to PFP, HNP, or CP leaders who feel that the full range of state authority, including the SADF, is engaged not only in maintaining the regime, but in furthering NP policy and partisan ends. In the words of Koos van der Merwe, CP defense spokesman, "the Minister of Defence, typical of so many other National Party politicians, is now using the total onslaught against South Africa as a weapon against the NP's political opponents in an attempt to win cheap political points."[32] Seen from this vantage, little can be done to set this mind at ease. Ironically, government gets criticized by the PFP for using the SADF to resist significant social change and by the HNP and the CP for jeopardizing the security of the state by changing the system too rapidly. Such flack from both positions need not, however, serve to exonerate the government from either criticism or both.

Constitutional change and reform would seem to be one policy area the SADF would want to influence. Although it stands to reason that SADF thinkers, as individuals and even as a group, would prefer to establish a constitutional order that they would feel more comfortable furthering and defending, there is no evidence of direct SADF input in the deliberations of the Constitutional Committee of the President's Council.

V. THE ECONOMY

Self-sufficiency in weaponry and military material quite obviously is the proper concern of the state security planners. It is also related to the strength and coordination of the national economy and infrastructure, and these, in turn, are linked to the machinery of the state. Because of these imperatives it is likely that the regime will also feel compelled to achieve greater economic self-sufficiency, even at the expense of higher short-range economic prices. After all, if outright warfare is contemplated, why would subviolent hostile acts such as sanctions and embargoes not also be possible? Some industries are undeniably related to the military defense of the system. Steel, energy, transport, automotive, chemical, food, and other related industries come to mind. Likewise, manpower and even educational matters have direct economic and security consequences. Small wonder that the SSC, the SADF, and other components of the security establishment should seek to become involved in decisions in these policy areas and many others. Armscor and other links between the economy and the state have already been discussed.

Much of the effort to acquire or develop nuclear technologies and capacities has an obvious military and foreign policy application. The same might be said of the expansion of Sasol facilities in order to enhance the country's self-sufficiency in petrol energies. Most of the other economic efforts are more remote, temporally, from a direct military or defensive utility.

Nonetheless, this does not deter security policymakers from being alert to the long-range necessity of developing a self-reliant economy. During the debate and discussion of the local-content program of the automotive industry, for example, the fear of sanctions and an awareness of military linkages were frequently expressed.[33] For example, radial tires for large trucks are now manufactured locally, apparently as a direct result of the development of radials for operational military vehicles.[34]

In addition, the military helped to persuade government that South Africa needed its own diesel capacity. In 1978 the government decided to let out bids for a diesel industry for South Africa. But, since diesel manufacturing is a high-technology, precision-machinery industry requiring high tolerances, South Africa now produces diesel engines at around one-third greater cost than imported models. Many industrialists and economists predicted this outcome. Higher costs, obsolete designs that are less fuel efficient, and totally South African financing have led to a situation in which South Africa is not really self-sufficient, since licensing is still required. It was apparent, however, that through the preparations for this decision, the SADF and the strategic planners would not be satisfied with anything less than 100 percent South African diesels—even if it could be demonstrated that there was, say, a 90 percent chance of South Africa being able to continue to import diesel engines. The government later admitted that the decision had been 80 percent strategic and 20 percent economic. Louis Wilking, managing director of General Motors (SA), wryly quipped: "It looks more to me like it is 111 percent strategic and minus 20 percent economic." Others criticized the decision as well, including the chief economic advisor to the prime minister.[35] Sure enough, in his 1984 Defence white paper, the minister boasted that "after 2 years of planning, testing and preparation all operational vehicles are being equipped with locally assembled diesel engines as from 1984."[36]

In those fields where total self-sufficiency is not approachable, the government has coopted many foreign firms into security collaboration. The National Key Points Act of 1980, the Atomic Energy Act as amended, the National Supplies Procurement Act as amended, and the Petroleum Products Amendment Act, among other pieces of legislation, require private firms to maintain secrecy about their production levels, sources of supply, trading partners, and so forth, and this contributes to the siege mentality. Such legislation also compromises branch subsidiaries of transnational firms with corporate headquarters outside South Africa. It is likely, however, that few foreign firms resist such strictures provided the costs are kept tolerable and total corporate operations are not too adversely affected.[37] One could also surmise that in this environment there is a good deal of planning and implementation of secret stockpiles, strategic reserves, and contingency plans entangling the private sector and the strategic planners. Likewise, when it comes to manpower allocation, both economists and strategists are deeply interested.

In another policy area there appears to be an uncanny confluence of strategic and economic thinking. This is the matter of regional economic planning and strategic/territorial planning. General Malan has frequently reminded his colleagues that "military preparedness is inseparable from economic strength."[38] This view is undoubtedly shared in the highest policy circles. The various industrial development plans, physical development plans, decentralization schemes, long-range homeland and national state consolidation plans, and regional military command boundaries virtually overlap at every turn. They could not have been delimited without close and high-level coordination. The 1980 Physical Development Plan of the SADF resulted directly from the National Physical Development Plan. Since then SADF units and installations have been sited where possible in accordance with the guidelines of the forty-four planning and eight development regions. The SADF claims that it is actively involved in all guide- and master-plan decisions for cities and towns in South Africa.[39] Again, there is nothing notably wrong or perverse about this. Indeed, it is rather farsighted to be able to show such purpose and organization. But it is further evidence of an order that values politico-strategic conformity and collaboration, and one that is structured to bring them about—a not insignificant achievement.

The military of the 1980s is, quite clearly, multidimensional. Unlike its 1960s counterpart, it is no longer just an instrument of coercion. Military officers are involved professionally in technology, education, anthropology, engineering, psychology, journalism, and the economy. Members of the officer corps are managers and technologists as much as they are soldiers in the traditional sense.

Despite the increased professionalization of the PF, it must be remembered that the SADF is to a large extent a part-time force. In 1984 career soldiers represented only 25.5 percent of the full-time force and a far smaller proportion of the ready forces.[40] With compulsory national service for white men, virtually every white family has been touched by the security demands of the state. In addition, Citizen Force and Commando units are more than military formations. They embody an ethic, particularly in the Afrikaner historical mystique.[41] The Bible and the gun are both part of the tradition of expansion and survival for the *volk*. Afrikaner values thereby infuse the armed forces just as military values are instilled in society. As a result, there is a closer than normal (for a westernized system) relationship between the armed forces and the white citizenry. Along with an inclination to accept and support the SADF there is also a willingness to criticize the professionals. In other words, white people are more closely involved with their armed forces. At the same time as there is a greater militarization of civilian life, there is a politicization of the military. How else could it be with an armed force that is, for white South Africa, a "peoples" force, a nation at arms? Government puts its trust in military power because whites want to trust their future to military power.

CHAPTER V

A Strategic Constellation of States and Policy Toward the Homelands

The encirclement of the Republic, brought on in large part by the Republic's own domestic racial order, requires that when one thinks of a "total national strategy" one conceives of it in at least regional terms. Events in neighboring states, in ostensibly independent homelands, and in self-governing homelands in various stages of domination, effect the total strategy. Their stability or instability, their economic achievements and frustrations, their evaluations of Pretoria's regime, become important data to be analyzed and influenced by the Republic. In short, in a state confronted by a "total onslaught," virtually everything foreign and domestic becomes a fitting subject for state policy and guidance.

I. PROBLEMS OF HOMELAND DEFENSE[1]

The territorial and administrative subdivision of what had been the RSA prior to the "independence" of the Transkei has important military ramifications. If one considers the hiving off of the homelands into "national states" with their dozens of parcels of territory as a problem of territorial and border defense, one can appreciate the apprehension and anxiety that military planners must feel. The independence of the Transkei, Bophuthatswana, Venda, and Ciskei alone have added 4,930 kilometers to South Africa's land borders.[2] Not that the national states or potential national states pose any immediate military threat to the Republic. Rather the multiplication of "international boundaries" and the prospects for governmental and social instabilities in these lands add to the potential problems that must be factored into strategic arrangements. To be sure, the SADF has been responsible for training and equipping homeland defense forces. Moreover, these regimes are economically dependent on the Republic, and their present governments will, for a long time to come, look to Pretoria for economic and military assistance, and even political maintenance.[3] But a future not entirely or directly in Pretoria's control complicates defense and foreign policy. An MP from the NRP put it most caustically when he condemned the homelands scheme as a "nightmare" for South Africa's military commanders. "Surely even a moron can see that this map is the most illogical and stupid plan ever devised by man."[4] But SADF is not alone in patrolling the borders. SAP is responsible for "internal" borders and the SADF for "external" borders, and SAP has its own highly regarded COIN units.

The debate over the homelands scheme is an old one, as United Party parliamentarians resisted the unfolding policy of homelands in the 1960s. Their leader, Sir de Villiers Graaff, asserted that the homelands policy showed "a total disregard for considerations of defence."[5] The UP catalogue of defense-related horrors bears repeating, as they noted that:

1) eight separate armies in eight separate homelands would open a Pandora's box of problems;

2) communist states might be involved in supplying arms and training to homeland armies;

3) terror gangs might operate from the homelands, thereby making the homelands "a festering sore on our borders in ten or twenty or thirty years time,"[6] much as Cuba became a threat to the United States;

4) revolutionary forces might seek to remove compliant pro-Pretoria regimes in the homelands and thus use their territories as "liberated areas";

5) the granting of independence to homelands would mean the surrender of South Africa's "entire defence perimeter" along all but the southern frontier to blacks who were years away from establishing "any adequate defence."[7] Transkei was thus seen as South Africa's "soft under-belly."

One could not be sure whether the defense of South Africa would be threatened by homeland independence because the homelands would be too weak or because they might be too strong or too independent.

The NP government countered in those days with assertions of confidence and assurances that the new black states would be so grateful for having been granted independence that a commonwealth would "arise." If South Africa were ever attacked, Verwoerd had said, the "common sense of the Bantu," and South Africa's "friendship" and "assistance" would lead the homelands to stand with South Africa.[8]

Certainly many of the UP fears have been borne out. By and large, however, the chief border issues have had little to do with revolutionaries, guerrillas, and unrest. These issues have centered around practical questions of stock theft, trespass, fences, and relocations of blacks.[9] For the South African government, however, the problems are seen as security issues. The governments in all the "independent" homelands, except for the Mangope government in Bophuthatswana, have been severely criticized on matters of human, political, and civil rights, and have been none too secure. On more than one occasion, Pretoria has felt the need to assist homeland governments in jeopardy. For example, since its nominal independence in December 1981, the Ciskeian government has been faced with strong, vocal, and organized opposition from a nascent trade union movement in Mdantsane, outside of East London. The Sebe government has regularly used strong-arm tactics and repressive emergency provisions to put down its foes. In 1983, while President Lennox Sebe was travelling to Israel, South African intelligence reportedly informed him of an imminent political coup in the Ciskei.[10] Sebe terminated his trip, and with the assistance of the SAP arrested the suspected coup leaders. These included Charles Sebe, the president's brother, and at the time the head of the Ciskei police, army, and national intelligence service. His second-in-command, Taillefer Minnaar, a white South African and former SADF officer, was also arrested, as were a number of Sebe's closest aides. To underscore this supportive link, South Africa's two highest-ranking police officers visited Ciskei immediately following the detentions. The brutal behavior of Ciskei's security apparatus, before and since Charles Sebe's removal, punctuates the vulnerability of the homelands to unrest and instability. Similar unpopular governments and seedbeds of violence exist in Venda and Transkei.[11] They become, then, not a tool for South African security policy, but a problem against which South Africa must constantly be on guard. That South Africa must expend forces or resources to prop up unpopular regimes hardly can please the SAP and the SADF with the overall prognosis of the homelands policy. So far, unrest in the independent "national states" has not required the deployment of regular SADF or SAP formations, but the prospects for long-range stability do not look promising, and strategic planners in Pretoria must be less than satisfied with a situation beyond their direct control.

The fear that outside powers might seek to become involved in the region or in South African affairs by means of the homelands has also been broached. So far no communist states have become implicated as the UP earlier had suggested. But Israel is reported to be supplying the Ciskei with aircraft and instructors and Nigeria, it is claimed, had nearly become involved with the Transkei Defence Force.[12] The white regime in Rhodesia also dabbled in homeland military affairs. Thus the precedent had been set that a foreign government, without formally recognizing a homeland, might secretly assist it militarily. Presumably Pretoria is prepared to exercise an effective veto on any such arrangement should it decide that the arrangement is threatening to South Africa's interests.

But the obvious necessity is to assure that the homelands are ruled by politicians friendly to Pretoria. Conceivably the homelands do have the potential for becoming hotbeds of antiapartheid activities, much as Palestinian refugee camps became problems for the Israeli and Lebanese governments. For as long as the homelands lack economic viability, for as long as they are overpopulated, for as long as their governments fail to represent their peoples, their miseries will spill over into South Africa. By various means, Pretoria is determined to prevent this from happening. Government thinkers and strategic planners currently seem less inclined to leave the matter to chance and more intent on developing policies to offset any potential threat. But they seem unwilling to address the central issue itself, the economic exploitation inherent in racial and territorial separation.

The extent to which SADF thinkers agree with government on the question of homeland policy is difficult to ascertain, and in many respects it is not that important. Certainly, these thinkers would probably subscribe to the necessity of keeping rural blacks separate from urban blacks in order to avoid the future need for simultaneous COIN operations in both sectors. Whether they concur that the present model of homeland self-government and eventual independence facilitates that end is not clear. One must surmise that it would be difficult for them to be pleased with the current conceptualization of homelands in all its particulars.

Defense of the homelands, in other words, is contingent on the pursuit of a homelands policy the precise parameters of which are still unclear. Efforts to provide some greater strategic assurance have taken a number of paths, each of which might be pursued independently, but together might produce a consistent package that would expedite state security for the RSA and for the particular homeland governments in question.

The multiple components of strategic policy on this issue are challenging to integrate. To begin, the SADF is committed to creating, training, and maintaining in material the defense forces for each homeland as it acquires "independence."[13] As each homeland follows "the road of independence to its end" it will establish its own "military unit in one form or another." If one accepts the premise that these noncontinguous territorial patches are to become parts of sovereign and fully independent states, then it would have to follow that their governments would be sovereign and free to pursue defense and foreign policies in their own interests as they perceive them.

The homeland defense forces, in turn, are regarded by Pretoria as integral parts of the larger regional defense scheme, although it is difficult for an outsider to grasp the precise configuration of that scheme as contemplated in Pretoria. Government spokesmen have repeatedly referred to regional defense as if they see the larger picture in explicit terms. Although homelands have gained what Pretoria calls independence, the homelands still occupy a position within "the military milieu of the Republic of South Africa and not outside the military milieu of the Republic of South Africa."[14] Strategically Pretoria wants to eat its cake and have it, too. Just how an independent state is to be required to have its defense policy conform to that of the Republic is not publicly specified, but politically and economically it is more than possible—it is likely.

These sorts of issues were raised anew when the government of the Transkei severed diplomatic and military relations with South Africa in 1978—at the time a theatrical act, but in practical terms inconsequential. Despite the embarrassments and obstacles these questions entail, Pretoria continues to regard homeland armies as part of the southern African defense system arrayed against the onslaught of Marxism and communist imperialism. With the government's resurrection of the idea of a regional constellation or confederation of states, the SADF again is called upon to design and promote a means for joint defense of the region. SADF personnel on secondment or ex-SADF members continue to occupy high-level positions in the forces of all the homelands except Transkei and Ciskei. In Transkei ex-Rhodesians prevail. In Ciskei, so far, the South Africans have not been replaced. They had been withdrawn by South Africa in January 1985 following the suspension by the Sebe government of the commander of the Ciskei Defence Force, a seconded SADF officer, and two of his colleagues. In all, about fifty South Africans left the Ciskeian forces.

II. REGIONAL FORMATIONS FOR SOUTH AFRICA'S BLACK PEOPLES

When the SADF first began to use black African volunteer soldiers, they were grouped into a single battalion (the 21) composed of men from several ethnic and linguistic groups. Eventually 21 Battalion was transformed into a training school and elite unit. But when it came to providing for the larger manpower needs of the Defence Force, it was decided to establish a number of "regional" units (each composed of a single language group). Each is attached to a regional command. Regional units so structured would fit well into the evolving model for "area defence." If more of the white citizenry is to be drawn into the defense picture by being subject to special call-up to defend their immediate regions, why not also engage local blacks? Blacks "have to help us [the SADF] spread a geographic presence and to maintain it." Thus the regional companies, said Deputy Minister of Defence H.J. Coetsee, "fulfill the role of a military presence, the showing of the flag, in a specific region."[15]

But the experiment has not proven altogether successful. Some units (for example, the Zulu 121 Battalion) have had recruitment problems and difficulties interacting with the homeland authorities. The result is that the SADF has moved more cautiously into black recruitment than had originally been planned.

The establishment of regional-cum-ethnic units helps flesh out a complex picture of organizational diversity toward a single end. Initially four such "battalions"/companies were established in 1979. It was over a year later before official announcement of their existence was made (May 1980). In fact, the first four regional units did not fare as well as hoped. It appears that the ambitious plans to create eighteen such formations have been delayed or shelved. Originally, these regional formations were seen as embryonic homeland armies, to be attached to each new "national state" upon its independence. But in fact the SADF established both a Venda National Force as well as a distinct 112 Battalion for Venda volunteers. And many Venda in the 21 Battalion (multiethnic) and in the 112 Battalion were not pleased by the prospect of leaving the SADF for a career in the VNF. It was not until September 1982 that the Venda government took charge of the 112 Battalion.

The KwaZulu government will have nothing officially to do with the 121 (Zulu) Battalion, and apparently force levels of the battalion have dropped after an initial growth. The status of the 113 (Shangaan) and 111 (Swazi) Battalions is unclear, especially in light of the KaNgwane-Ingwavuma land issues. In 1984 a start was made in training Ndebeles for a KwaNdebele regional unit, the nucleus of an army for that homeland.

In the final analysis, the reversion to regional/ethnic units is an atavism, a return to ideological thinking in group and racial terms. Not that there ever was a departure from this mode. The short-lived experiment with broader groupings such as the 21 Battalion has not been enlarged. Traditional thinking at SADF headquarters seems to have prevailed over "progressive" thinking. With the falling off of immediate defense needs and presumably the slowdown in the creation of even the ethnic units, even that element of change has been arrested.

III. JOINT STRATEGIC SCHEMES: MONROE AND BREZHNEV REVIVED

A NATO-type alliance is unattainable. More likely some version of a Brezhnev or Monroe doctrine may be in the cards—one that correctly accounts for the military asymmetries that exist and which may be brought into play unilaterally. The SADF would like to exercise a "right of access" and joint command arrangement in times of emergency—not that any such formalities would be required as demonstrated by the extensive preemptive cross-border operations on the Republic's northern frontiers.

Certainly joint security planning is the lowest common denominator to be expected. By and large most planning efforts involving Pretoria and the homeland governments deal with issues other than strategy. There are bilateral joint defense management councils or committees and quite probably a multilateral working committee for security, although the long-festering Ciskei-Transkei animosity would complicate that. One suspects that discussions tend to address narrow functional or housekeeping chores, such as training, weapons standardization and supply, security intelligence exchange, and so forth. Insofar as there is strategic planning regarding joint homeland/RSA questions, it is to all intents and purposes the exclusive purview of the SADF, sovereignty and independence notwithstanding. Under P.W. Botha at Defence, the SADF was trusted and assigned principal responsibility for negotiating with the homeland governments on defense collaboration. Details were not the concern of Foreign Affairs, for example. P.W. Botha has displayed this attitude throughout his tenure. In his view, the upper echelon of the SADF is trustworthy as well as sensitive to political and diplomatic concerns. This view, however, is not shared by all policymakers in the South African hierarchy.

IV. TERRITORIAL ADJUSTMENTS

The heart of the problem is perceived by many to be territorial or spatial. Thus the sheer number of strategic difficulties could be reduced if only the homelands were more compact and contiguous, thereby rendering fewer and shorter boundaries for the security forces to "defend." As early as 1974, Brigadier C.L. Viljoen, then director of operations for the Army, suggested that the consolidation of the homelands would be beneficial from a security standpoint. He contended that the existing fragmentation was militarily unacceptable.[16] The van der Walt Commission (the Central Consolidation Commission appointed in 1979) deals with homeland consolidation. It has come to realize that decisions regarding parcels of land have military ramifications, as logistical problems are compounded by the reassignment of roads, bridges, and other transport infrastructure. The air radar network might be weakened as parcels of land are moved from the Republic to the homelands. The proximity of homelands to cities might also be viewed critically by the police and other security arms. For these reasons, among others, the SADF is represented on the commission and can thereby seek to make the commission aware of the possible dangers and opportunities of particular consolidation proposals. And when specific pieces of property are discussed at meetings of farmers, SADF officers often attend to allay the farmers' fears.[17]

In other ways, border adjustments and territorial grants to neighboring states might also be seen as having a strategic dimension. Homelands tend to occupy strategic territory on or near South Africa's borders.[18] They form a semicircle around the industrial and mining heartland of the Republic. Moreover, these territories are generally inhabited by ethnic elements that also live in independent neighboring countries. Such a

situation is a two-edged sword, as the histories of the non-Russian mi-
norities of the Soviet Union indicate. Spillover ethnic groups pose problems, but they also widen the foreign policy and strategic options.

Historical claims based on ethnic occupation were at the base of the
Transkei's justification for its severance of diplomatic relations with South
Africa in 1978 and its abrogation of the nonaggression pact and military
training and cooperation agreements. There were other reasons for their
actions, but when international recognition and support were not forthcoming and the Transkei's abject dependence on South Africa became
apparent and awkward to deny, the Transkei ended its foray into con-
frontational politics. Diplomatic relations with Pretoria were resumed.
Interestingly, the Transkei justified its retreat by stressing South Africa's
expressed willingness to negotiate the Transkei's demands that South
Africa transfer East Griqualand to the Transkei.[19]

One way of understanding these territorial relationships is to see them
as a series of concentric security circles.[20] The inner circle or core consists
of the so-called white parts of South Africa. Here the central government
is singularly responsible for security and defense. The innermost ring
would then consist of those homelands that have not gained or even
sought independence. Here might be included, for examples, KwaZulu,
QwaQwa, and Gazankulu. The "boundaries" in this instance are porous
and, in fact, when it comes to security, the Pretoria government is legally
and politically responsible for defense and the maintenance of law and
order in these entities. The second ring, more remote from the inner
core, are those homelands that have opted for, or have been granted,
"independence." Here the security links with Pretoria are more tenuous
and diverse, especially before, but also since, the act of independence.
For a variety of economic and political reasons the Republic sees these
territories as a part of the larger regional security system. It is not an
association of equals by any means.

It appears that the National Party government would like to transform
the homelands, as each acquires independence, into a second ring of
buffer states to replace what had been a defense in depth prior to the fall
of the Portuguese in Africa and the Zimbabwe transfer of power. As a
first and rather ineffectual line of defense against insurgents, the bantustan
armies pose little more than token resistance. Still they are important.
They are the trip-hammer that activates contingency plans in which the
homeland governments invite in the SADF. The security of the two
regimes, Pretoria's and the homelands', are inextricably interwoven, as
successive South African governments have structured the situation.

Pretoria's policies have been inconsistent and most baffling in some
cases. Not that consistency is either wise or practical. In two instances,

Transkei and Bophuthatswana, homelands gained their independence with territory flush against an international border. In the Venda case a narrow strip of territory was excised and retained by the Republic, and the inhabitants thereof were relocated into Venda. In still other instances attempts were made to transfer the territory of an entire homeland or a major part of one to an independent neighboring state (KaNgwane and KwaZulu). In short, if there is a method to this madness, it is cryptic at the least. The common denominators are Pretoria's desires to rid itself of black population otherwise able to claim South African citizenship and to do what is necessary to stabilize homeland governments when they are friendly to Pretoria. If homelands are to constitute a kind of cordon sanitaire, why did Pretoria with the consent of the Venda authorities push for a five kilometer-wide strip of land between Venda and the Limpopo River? A similar question might be asked of the effort to grant KaNgwane and Ingwavuma to Swaziland. By removing Venda from direct contact with the Zimbabwe border, or KaNgwane and Ingwavuma from the Swaziland and Mozambican borders, the buffer principle falls away. Factually, one might argue that the homelands were never well suited to serve as protective buffers. But the homelands on the international borders had been dealt with inconsistently, and it is hard to discern just what strategic role they are expected to perform.

It had been the dream of Swaziland's King Sobuza II to unite all Swazis under a single government, namely his Swaziland. His were aspirations based on traditional and historical experience, or so it has been argued. To accommodate the king, we have been told, and most probably for a variety of other reasons, Pretoria was prepared to cede to Swaziland all of the KaNgwane (Swazi) homeland and the Ingwavuma region of KwaZulu. KaNgwane is a homeland around fifty-six miles long and from three to twelve miles wide along Swaziland's northern and western borders with South Africa. It contains around 250,000 Swazi people and possesses no known viable natural resources. Ingwavuma is now part of KwaZulu, and runs from Swaziland to the Indian Ocean along the South African border with Mozambique. Pretoria's offer to divest itself of part of the Zulu heritage enraged Chief Gatsha Buthelezi. Although the outcome, details, and larger questions need not concern us here, Pretoria knows full well that boundary disputes and unfulfilled irredentas are unresolved causes of dispute, even between unequal parties. Transkeian and Ciskeian land claims, vast Lesotho claims including the QwaQwa homeland, Venda claims, and other discontents might be seen as subject to territorial adjustments and transfers. Decisions, especially controversial ones, like the territorial exchange schemes involving Swaziland, are not taken lightly or without considerable domestic political bloodletting. The

idea of ceding large pieces of South African territory to a neighboring
state does not go down easily with committed nationalists (small *n* or
capital, black or white).

The manner in which the land cession was decided (unilaterally and in
camera) and announced (ambiguously and disingenuously) added to a
distrustful sense that there must be another, secret agenda that Pretoria
and Mbabane were not publicizing. Strong opposition from other quarters, foreign and domestic, white and black, governmental supporters
and those hostile to the government, mounted. It was assumed that a
substantial quid pro quo must have been expected to offset the likely
political costs.

The geostrategic issues, although not widely regarded as particularly
crucial to their decision, were likely considered, even though the prima
facie evidence seemed to suggest that they were not important. A case
can be made that important security factors were overlooked or down
played. Swaziland's stability and economic progress could be threatened
by the addition of some 800,000 more inhabitants, not all of whom are
Swazi and large numbers who do not want to lose their South African
citizenship or become citizens of Swaziland. Given the king's age at the
time of the announcement, a succession struggle combined with the
unwieldy assimilation of people who would then constitute over 60 percent
of the country's total population might simply be indigestible. At that
time the bulk of ANC infiltrators into the Republic passed through Swaziland. So ceding more territory to Swaziland (some one million hectares)
hardly augered well for border region security. White farmers in northern
Natal and the Lowveld informed Pretoria of their fears. The thinly pop-
ulated Ingwavuma region would not be easily policed either.

Another strategic dimension would involve providing Swaziland with
its own outlet to the sea and with the opportunity to develop a port at
Kosi Bay. Rumors circulated that the United States, anxious to counter
Soviet naval power in the Indian Ocean and for political reasons unwilling
to utilize South African ports or to develop naval facilities in a homeland
thereby tacitly associating with the policy of separate development, might
have been willing to invest heavily at Kosi Bay if it were part of Swaziland.
Denials of this line of reasoning have been firm.

No need to speculate further as to why the scheme was hatched. Those
identified with the scheme suffered politically. Pik Botha in Foreign
Affairs and Dr. Piet Koornhof, minister of cooperation and development,
were burnt in terms of intraparty maneuvering. In contrast to the speed
with which the land deal was announced in June 1982, one got the
impression that it was not such a spur-of-the-moment idea. The Swaziland-
South Africa security agreement dating from February 1982 (but not made

public until 1984) contributes to this conclusion. It is also revealing that the Physical Development Plan map for the Republic and surrounding lands clearly placed Ingwavuma and KaNgwane *outside* the Republic's borders and made them a part of Swaziland. It had been printed before the land deal was announced. The proposed Industrial Development Plan, in contrast, depicts them as part of South Africa.

According to one account this scheme originated with the secretariat of the SSC. In order to try to entice Swaziland to cooperate with con- stellation/confederation and to encourage Swaziland to serve as a link between SADCC (the Southern African Development Coordination Con- ference) and any embryonic constellation involving the Republic, it was proposed that KaNgwane be offered to Swaziland. Ingwavuma was alleg- edly not a part of the original design. This proposal was then supposedly turned over to the appropriate cabinet committee, where both the foreign minister and the minister for cooperation and development could better coordinate their efforts. The strategic planners proposed—the politicians disposed in a manner not at all to the liking of the military thinkers at the SSC secretariat. If this account is accurate, and confirmation is vir- tually impossible, then indeed the security establishment has a central role in foreign affairs and in other issues outside strictly strategic matters.

But Defence does not always carry the day. The DFAI, which would be the state department that would normally handle relations with Swa- ziland, and the Department of Cooperation and Development, the agency in charge of homeland affairs, have been embarrassed and upstaged in a policy area that has eluded their principal direction.

Not until March 1984, after the momentum had been initiated in agreements with Mozambique and Angola and accommodation seemed possible with Zimbabwe and Lesotho, was it announced that, in fact, South Africa and Swaziland had entered into a security agreement, fully two years earlier and just before the KaNgwane-Ingwavuma land deal had been announced. That agreement came into being through an ex- change of notes. After an introductory paragraph expressing the awareness of the two parties that international "terrorism" poses a threat to peace and security, the states agreed to undertake to combat "terrorism, in- surgency and subversion" individually and collectively, and to call on each other for assistance to eliminate this evil. They also agreed not to allow within their respective territories any activities which are directed toward the commission of any act involving a threat or use of force against each other's territorial integrity. The two governments are also required not to allow the installation or maintenance of foreign military bases or the presence of foreign military units within their respective territories except in accordance with their right of self-defense in the event of armed

attack and only after due notification to the other.[21] It is significant that
the two governments chose to remain silent until the political climate in
the region became more conducive to disclosure. It is just as significant
that the disclosure appeared calculated to pressure other governments in
the region to enter into similar agreements.

Surely there are historical territorial claims that one might consider in
assessing the Pretoria-Mbabane line.[22] But it would appear, after the fact,
that the KaNgwane-Ingwavuma land deal was very much based on the
blossoming strategic links between the two governments. In retrospect,
it can be seen that the timing of the Swazi government's action against
the ANC would confirm this assertion. A Swazi crackdown on ANC
activities within Swaziland began early in 1982. The longstanding ANC
representative in the country was forced to leave, frequent raids on
suspected ANC houses were launched, and laws were tightened regarding
the possession of "arms of war." ANC operatives were rounded up and
detained, others were forced to flee "voluntarily" to Mozambique. The
overall impact was to cripple the ANC in Swaziland. The timing of these
acts was more than coincidence. Swaziland, under mounting pressure
from the Botha Government, joined South Africa in combatting the "Marxist" threat to the region. By 1984 Swaziland's patience was almost expended, as the government threatened to expel all ANC members from
the country.[23]

The territorial issues were finally settled in June 1984, when Dr. P.G.J.
Koornhof announced that the South African government had abandoned
the plan to cede KaNgwane and Ingwavuma to Swaziland.[24] The proposed
land deal had been announced in June 1982. In August King Sobhuza
died at the age of eighty-three. The initial declaration by Minister Koornhof to the KwaZulu Legislative Assembly brought an outcry of protest
from a wide spectrum of black and white political groups.

Immediately legal obstacles were placed in the way of the consum-
mation of the deal. In October 1982 the Appeal Court upheld the KwaZulu
government's contention that the proclamation was unlawful, and in November Pretoria announced that it had accepted the court's decision and
had also settled with the KaNgwane government by withdrawing its
transfer proclamation. The South African government decided to refer
the problem to a commission to investigate the rival claims of all parties.
Although the Swazi government continues to express interest in pursuing
the land cessions, Pretoria must have felt that the new atmosphere in the
region, especially regarding Mozambique no longer required these particular territorial changes. In June 1984 the South African government
dissolved the Commission of Inquiry, and in August, as final evidence
that Pretoria had abandoned the land deal, South Africa granted internal
"self-government" to KaNgwane.

V. TREATIES OF NONAGGRESSION

Partly as an international as well as a regional public relations effort, partly
in order to establish the legal and ideological bases for greater military
cooperation, partly to legitimize its regional hegemony, and partly to
facilitate improved relations with neighboring states and territories, the
Republic has offered to negotiate nonaggression pacts with all regional
states. When the idea was first advanced by J.B. Vorster in 1970, South
Africa had hoped to engage independent black states that were members
of the OAU. This was, at that time of course, a scheme that few took
seriously. The ideological chasm looked too wide. But equally prominent
in the rhetoric have been South African threats to retaliate should neighboring states harbor South African insurgents. And rhetoric was punc-
tuated with action. It was the latter instruction, the message of threat,
the world choose to hear. It was a message repeatedly reinforced by South
Africa's military invasions and forays. Black Africa's sense of reality is
more attuned to regional experience than to professions of nonaggressive
intentions emanating from the DFAI. Prior to late 1983 and early 1984,
only the former homeland governments had entered into such agreements, or so it seemed then. South Africa had concluded a series of
bilateral pacts with each of the four "independent" homelands, most likely
as nearly compulsory terms for their own achievement of independence.

No recognized independent states would then entertain the prospect,
at least publicly, of a cooperative military association or nonaggression
pact with South Africa. Any open political bond with the Republic was
regarded as a stigma too gruesome to contemplate. What is more, a
military treaty implies the acceptance of the political status quo. But
persistent military and economic pressure mounted by South Africa eventually did alter the situation in the region, and states long scornful of any
association with Pretoria found their policy options so constrained that
they had to deal with South Africa. The Nkomati accord and the cease-
fire in Angola opened a floodgate of speculation on where accommodation
might end.

The bilateral nonaggression pacts between Transkei, Bophuthatswana,
Venda, and Ciskei and South Africa were just the first plausible steps in
this direction. They are fairly elementary documents in which each party
pledges not to resort to the use of armed force against the territorial
sovereignty and political independence of the other. Article 2 is a bit
more portentous; it states that neither party shall allow its territory or
airspace to be used as a base or thoroughfare by any state, government,
organization, or person for military, subversive, or hostile actions or
activities against the other party. This commits each to a more positive
act of preventing such activity. Should a homeland government find itself

unable to enforce its undertaking as per Article 2, that might provide an excuse and legal basis for South African intervention, or it might prompt an invitation to South African forces by a government in fear that it might be losing control. These pacts do not oblige the parties to come to one another's defense when the security of one is threatened. A nonaggression pact, as innocuous as it may at first appear, can be a useful tool in the hands of an activist government.[25]

If the homelands, as they gain nominal independence, are to serve as buffers shielding the Republic militarily, some device or plan must be developed by which the Republic can rationalize its own right to intervene in neighboring territories when it perceives it is useful to do so. Economically and militarily the Republic is as dominant in southern Africa as is the United States in Latin America or the Soviet Union in Eastern Europe. Although superficially it may appear to be anathema for NP leaders to think about legitimizing their hegemony, some version of a Brezhnev or a Monroe doctrine may be evolved formalizing the Republic's relations with its homelands and with other neighbors. Apparently General J.C. Smuts advocated a Monroe doctrine in 1918 as a shield for Africa against European, and chiefly German, militarism.[26] More recently such ideas have been suggested to counter perceived threats from the Soviet Union and the Chinese Peoples Republic, but they have been more restricted regionally or even just to security links with the homelands.

Hence the Brezhnev doctrine comes more to mind with its declaration of limited sovereignty and justifications for intervention to maintain in power compatible socio-political systems. When the Brezhnev doctrine was propounded in 1968, it was an ex post facto rationalization for the Soviet-cum-Warsaw Pact intervention in Czechoslovakia. In that crisis involving a regional grouping of ostensibly independent states, the USSR contended that a member of the group enjoyed only limited sovereignty. Consequently, fraternal allies could intervene when the partner's class solidarity was endangered. The group, acting cooperatively and "by way of self-defense," claimed the right to use force to assure fraternal socialist unity and to prevent the possible collapse or overthrow of a member state's government. In reality, the rule of *collective* intervention to assure minimum standards of governmental conduct is asserted by the dominant regional actor. This is the basis of the Brezhnev doctrine and, if it is brought about, the basis of one version of a Pax Pretoriana.[27]

Insofar as there already is a serious question about the sovereignty of the homeland governments—and in that group solidarity has not, as yet, been institutionalized or formalized à la the Warsaw Pact—such a doctrine might more readily be applied toward a homeland government than, say, in a situation where there is no doubt about the juridical sovereign independence of the state. Clearly, Pretoria feels that it must have the right to intervene preventatively, "preemptive intervention" they call it, when necessary, in any part of its former territory if its interests should be threatened. The task is to devise an instrument and salable rationale for the expression of that proclaimed right.[28]

VI. CONFEDERATION AND CONSTELLATION

The creation of a confederation of southern African states such as proposed by the Botha Government could expedite such a desire, yet so far the constellation/confederation idea has been most openly applied to economic and functional interaction, not to military/security links. Although it may be Pretoria's policy to regard the homeland security forces as part of a collaborative regional defense system to fight together against the Marxist onslaught, their anticipated role may be little more than the canary in the coal mine—to signal to the SADF that larger-scale action must be taken to stem the tide of opposition to a homeland government and to the larger apartheid system. So far no homeland has secured any form of diplomatic recognition except by Pretoria. Therefore, intervention, by invitation or without, would be relatively risk free. It would also corroborate the rest of the world's rejection of the fruits of separate development.

The idea of constellation/confederation is the brainchild of Foreign Affairs and the South African economic establishment. If neighboring states can be enmeshed in an economic network, expanded to include functional and even diplomatic ties, then military operations become less likely and necessary. Structural control is superior to coercive control— and cheaper. The specifics of various constellation/confederation structures are not important to this discussion.[29] Total strategy requires the creation of some form of confederation, at minimum involving independent and nonindependent homelands, and maximally including regional neighbors that belong to the OAU. If carried to its logical conclusion, cooperation and interaction today might lead in a stage-like progression to a reintegration into a confederation and eventually to a federation of diverse national states. In this fashion, the ultimate vision might be to reconnect what the Verwoerdian paradigm sought to tear asunder. White South Africa is still dominant. Confederation becomes a "second prize" of sorts for South Africa's blacks, understandably disheartened by their exclusion from the body politic and from the new constitutional dispensation. Bear in mind that the political, ideological, and economic conflicts of interest and the asymmetries of power between South Africa and its neighbors cannot be wished away by assuming that shared economic realities can heal all breaches. Black southern African leaders are more realistic than Pretoria's spokesmen care to admit.

There is another strategic dimension to the idea of constellation. Prime Minister Botha has mentioned security as an important field for constellation cooperation.[30] Whether this can be taken to mean that a series of bilateral pacts between the Republic and the homelands is inadequate to Pretoria's needs is not clear. The Warsaw Pact is also a series of bilateral treaties with Moscow at the center of each, and this arrangement has not hampered "fraternal" socialist military policy. It has been suggested that South Africa and the homelands should formalize and institutionalize security cooperation through regular ministerial meetings and through the establishment of a multilateral security committee of high-level governmental respresentatives. Thus, through regularized practice the need might be clear to multilateralize the bilateral treaties, and closer security ties would evolve. Such an alteration of current practices, however, merely complicates and unduly obligates Pretoria. The current bilateral ties are more than adequate for Pretoria to deal with the threat as presently posed.

The wider constellation involving bona fide sovereign neighbors is "dead," or so it would seem. South Africa's coercive activities may yet force black states to cooperate openly in some economic schemes, but then such links would be seen for what they were, unequal ties predicated on coercion and desperation. In those cases they would be manifestly unstable and transitory. Constellation has been a concept long associated with Pik Botha. When the design for CONSAS was announced, even before the Zimbabwean elections, it seemed a scheme to strengthen the Muzorewa forces in the forthcoming voting. But Pik was also pushing to steal the march on the military and their hawkish views on foreign policy. He might have been thinking that if he could usher in a cooperative government in Zimbabwe it might strengthen his hand in cabinet and in the SSC. He was, as one analyst put it, "prepared to barter the future in order to secure the Zimbabwe he wanted." He failed. It was premature to announce a constellation, and Mugabe's victory contributed to Pik being outmaneuvered in domestic party councils.

So Pretoria had to settle for the "minimal" constellation. Pretoria engaged client states that had no other possible partners and no way of escaping Pretoria's orbit. Now that Mozambique has signed the Nkomati accord—an agreement on nonaggression and good neighborliness—and has reactivated the Cahora Bassa contract, and now that Angola has agreed to a cease fire, and a settlement appears to be in the offing on Namibia, optimists in South Africa are again dusting off old ideas about detente, the outward foreign policy, and a maximalist constellation. South Africa seems ready to cremate SADCC and to bring forth a phoenix constellation in its place. But SADCC is not dead or even dying, and the real interests of the governments in black southern Africa do not admit of legitimating Pretoria's military and economic dominance. To accept the realities of the obvious may make sense to logicians, but politics is not logical. It would mean surrendering one of the few levers that the black states possess—the ability to sanction an unequal relationship from which they struggle to free themselves.

For years about all that could be expected was confederation concentrating on the new "independent national states" carved out of the pre-1976 Republic. Even much of that progressed sub rosa and with difficulty. At each stage through the years, South Africa had been forced to scale down its vision of regional cooperation. This narrow construction represented a blow to Pik Botha, DFAI, and the economic regionalists keen on spinning an economic spider web of constraints based on what they erroneously contend is mutual self-interest. A setback for Foreign Affairs can be translated into a victory for Defence in the hierarchy of Pretoria's politics. In the current euphoria of agreements with Angola and Mozambique and in the talk of economic and political breakthroughs to the north,[31] it should not be lost that these "triumphs" have been largely the product of military determination,[32] natural bad fortune (the drought), and economic mismanagement in black Africa. Although Pik Botha and Foreign Affairs seem pleased to take credit for the "peace offensive," they would do well to remember that it grows out of the barrel of a gun. Conditions for long-term cooperation are not there. But there are still hopes, one suspects, to parlay the bilateral nonaggression pacts into a more positive and assertive multilateral arrangement, perhaps even an outright alliance. That would be the signal for Defence assuming an even greater role in the realm of foreign affairs.

CHAPTER VI

Foreign Policy

What emerges in part from the preceding discussion is a picture of the Department of Foreign Affairs and Information being eclipsed (at least prior to 1984) by other governmental departments and agencies, even on decisions directly touching on foreign policy. This displacement began in the Vorster years with the rise of BOSS and the Information Department and the personalities associated with them. DFA was outmaneuvered and later elements of the defense establishment outflanked DFA still further. Even today, when it appears as if South Africa's efforts to stabilize the region by striking diplomatic agreements with black states on its borders are ready to bear fruit, it must be realized that it was the SADF that provided the initiative and thrust, and eventually forced those governments to come to terms. Certainly the SADF is convinced of its own importance in the stabilization process. In their words, "forceful military action" has provided time to allow Africans to experience "the dangers of Russian involvement in their countries, as well as the suffering and retrogression that follows upon the revolutionary formula." In short, South Africa's black neighbors have had their "eyes opened to the dangers of Russian imperialism." By taking "firm action" and developing "a strong military potential," the SADF "has created a successful strategy of deterrence."[1] In other words, without the SADF it would have been impossible to begin the negotiations that led to the cease fire and to non-aggression pacts.

I. ANGOLA, 1975–1976

South Africa's decision to intervene in Angola before and immediately after that country's independence in November 1975 was hotly debated and divisive in high places.[2] Prior to the determination to intervene, General van den Bergh had provided much of the momentum for Vorster's efforts at detente and for the prime minister's reluctant consent to meet with leaders of OAU member-states.[3] Hilgard Muller had proven to be a lackluster foreign minister and certainly not one influential in the party or the government. He was not the sort to be a strong and effective advocate of departmental policy and assertiveness in NP counsels—not in comparison to van den Bergh, P.W. Botha, or Connie Mulder, each in his way headstrong and manipulative.

It came as no surprise, then, that when Government was faced with some very difficult decisions regarding policy in the unfolding Angolan civil war leading to independence, Muller would take a back seat and more forceful personalities would contest the wheel. At one point the foreign ministry did not even learn of the SADF's first major offensive into Angola until a Portuguese note of protest was handed to the South African ambassador in Lisbon.[4] Insofar as the policy dispute can be characterized as one between hawks and doves, it was Defence arrayed against BOSS and Foreign Affairs (particularly Secretary Brand Fourie and Ambassador Pik Botha), and Information playing a supportive role. Apparently as conditions shifted in the field the coalition of voices for or against deeper involvement or withdrawal shifted. In this context field conditions refer not only to the military situation in Angola itself, but also to the global diplomatic picture, and particularly the indecisive American position (especially a result of the interplay among diverse branches and organs of the U.S. government), the appeals of black states in Africa, the ebb and flow of independence movement support, OAU maneuvers, and other foreign military and diplomatic dabblings.

Pretoria did not appear to know what it wanted to do largely because no clear-cut policy direction was established. The same South Africans were not in control, to the same degree, at every stage of the decisional process. Contestants for power realized that their domestic bases for support rested on shifting foundations. It is not my place to argue here the whys and wherefores of the issue. Suffice it to note the effects on the decisional nexus during this period.

To begin, although Defence and the SADF were identified with a hawkish orientation, they were somewhat restrained in their policy advocacy. Apparently Military Intelligence, after approaching indirectly each of the Angolan liberation movements, concluded that an MPLA government in Luanda might threaten South Africa's security interests in Namibia. In June 1975 the SADF submitted to the minister a policy paper setting out South Africa's options and the implications of each. It then went from the minister of defense to the prime minister. It took Vorster months to arrive at a decision on the issue. In the meantime, the South African forces were engaged in southern Angola in a vacuum of policy direction. P.W. Botha, after consultations with Vorster, reportedly provided the SADF with interim guidance—if attacked by MPLA forces, drive them off decisively. According to Geldenhuys, "a political decision opening the door to offensive military operations in Angola had been taken, and the two principal (if not the only) political decision-makers who were to control South Africa's military involvement in the Angolan war . . . identified."[5]

Perhaps the decision makers were too inclined to believe their intelligence about MPLA weaknesses and UNITA-FNLA strengths. Perhaps they overestimated American commitment and underestimated Soviet intentions. For whatever reasons, they did advocate deeper involvement and more direct and unambiguous orders. But considering their call for a military invasion, they were temperate. Their initial large-scale strikes, Operations Zulu and Foxbat, demonstrated restraint in the number of South African troops deployed and the composition of the forces, consisting of a Bushman (San) battalion, a black FNLA battalion, and about 300 "advisors/instructors" and SADF officers and NCOs. Perhaps this reflected the compromise character of the decision and the conduct of the intervention, by which hawks secured the decision to attack provided the doves were mollified by a less intensive and extensive SADF deployment. In addition, there had been a hiatus of sorts between the two thrusts during which Pretoria considered withdrawing its forces from Angola. It was decided to stay. The escalation of South African involvement came after Angola's November 11th independence. The later operations, X-ray, Protea, Orange, and Askari, for examples, were more overtly South African exercises in terms of personnel, with up to 2000 SADF members eventually engaged.

Throughout that period, however, there were few if any doves among the South African military strategists. At least they appreciated that little could be gained by committing more South African troops without more tangible Western support. And when they came to realize that Western assistance would not be forthcoming, and that what had been a free-wheeling bush war had become more like a conventional war with long logistical lines, larger troop concentrations, rapidly deployed vehicle columns with heavier artillery and projectiles, and when the SADF thinkers realized that their Angolan allies and clients, UNITA and FNLA, especially the latter, were ill-prepared for that kind of protracted struggle, the SADF leaders were willing, perhaps reluctantly, to pull back to more defensible positions (militarily and diplomatically).

The decision to retreat, that is to abandon the SADF's optional plan that included the capture of Luanda and to withdraw all forces except for border protection, was taken over the Christmas holiday during which the cabinet was unable to meet. The military hierarchy wanted to continue to aid FNLA and UNITA. The doves in BOSS and DFA argued that this military intervention was being used against South Africa and alienating many African and Western governments that earlier had not been particularly sympathetic to MPLA or a Cuban presence in Africa. Curiously, it was P. W. Botha who signaled a shift in government thinking when he stated, in effect, that South Africa would almost certainly reconsider its involvement in Angola if its interests in southern Angola were guaranteed and attacks into Namibia were terminated.[6]

Throughout the 1975–76 intervention, top military men felt tethered to a foreign policy that made their jobs awkward and difficult. During the crisis it was BOSS, not DFA, that kept communications open with black governments in Africa, and it was BOSS that was able to elicit discreet appeals from these governments to intervene and to stay in Angola.[7] It was BOSS as well that argued for withdrawal, and eventually BOSS got its way.

There are allegations of other major confrontations between P.W. Botha and van den Bergh that illustrate this mood of competition and distrust at the center.[8] After the Frelimo government seized power in Mozambique, Prime Minister Vorster took a conciliatory line (in contrast to his posture in the Angolan civil war). P.W. Botha, as minister of defense, took an opposing position and sought to support counterrevolutionary guerrillas trying to unseat President Machel. At the same time that Vorster had agreed to assist with the repair of Mozambique's railways and harbors, according to Dr. Eschel Rhoodie, Botha secretly ordered MIS to supply extensive quantities of arms and ammunition to guerrillas operating from a base near Komatipoort. When General van den Bergh learned of this he sent men to Nelspruit and Komatipoort to immobilize the equipment being transported to Mozambique. Botha also helped adopt the anti-Frelimo movement, *Resistência Nacional Moçambicana* (MNR or Renamo). MNR was first created by the Rhodesian Central Intelligence Organization (CIO) after Mozambique had gained its independence in 1975. It needed intelligence and subversion aimed at Robert Mugabe's forces based in Mozambique. When Zimbabwe won independence under Mugabe, the entire MNR structure was carted off to South Africa, where it became even more effective militarily and where SADF forces provided field assistance by means of "recce" groups. MNR, with considerable although denied South African support, was instrumental in driving the Machel government to the Nkomati agreement of 1984.

On another occasion immediately after the reputed withdrawal of SAP units from Rhodesia in 1975, Dr. Rhoodie has maintained that Botha arranged for 500 troops to be airlifted from Waterkloof Air Force Base to Rhodesia to help Ian Smith's security forces combat the Patriotic Front fighters. This coincided precisely with Vorster's assurances that South Africa was no longer directly involved in the Zimbabwean war. Again, at the eleventh hour, General van den Bergh told Vorster about Botha's designs and foiled Botha's plans. In all these dealings, it was DFA and especially the minister of foreign affairs, that was strangely silent or submissive. By adhering to the principle of noninterference in the domestic affairs of other countries, DFA was destined to clash with Defence, all too willing to take risks to prevent the MPLA's assumption of power. DFA effectively got its way in Mozambique policy. The SADF got its chance in Angola. Out of the crisis emerged BOSS and Information as Prime Minister Vorster's "second Department of Foreign Affairs" to offset the weight of Defence.

Interestingly, it was the Angolan issue with Defence arrayed against BOSS and DFA that probably led P.W. Botha to want to reorganize the entire foreign policy decision-making apparatus. South Africa lacked clear policy objectives in Angola, and thus it was awkward for the SADF to carry out policy and plan operations, the purposes of which were fuzzy or worse. This did not deter SADF from elaborate operational planning of "its" Angolan responsibility, but without political guidelines it must have been frustrating. When the information scandal broke and BOSS and Vorster plummeted from power, P.W. Botha was able to establish his new, more rationalized policy machinery.

The machinery in place for policymaking on the Angolan issue did not work well. It was ad hoc and idiosyncratic. In the end Vorster and Botha dominated. Parliament had virtually no role to play. Even the full cabinet met only after many of the vital decisions were taken. The State Security Council was conspicuously silent. Foreign Affairs frequently was excluded from the groups that made decisions. Intelligence, at least on the matter of the United States and on Cuban and MPLA policy, was unreliable. The National Party caucus was not consulted. It was the Vorster and P.W. Botha show with van den Bergh providing periodic shifts and tension. Such an arrangement could not be reliably counted on the next time crisis decision making was required. The process for regional and security decision making had to be structured.

II. NAMIBIA

South Africa's defense forces captured the foreign policy initiative, or at least through tactical activism framed policy or strategy by default. In May 1978 a massive strike against SWAPO bases in southern Angola, code-named Operation Reindeer, was the first large-scale military strike into Angola after the 1975–76 incursions. The "Reindeer" decision was P.W. Botha's revenge on the nonmilitary voices in the Party. Others in the SSC and in cabinet feared international repercussions, maybe even UN-sponsored sanctions. Defence carried the day. The raid was a military success and the diplomatic liabilities were contained. Operation Reindeer strengthened the security establishment in foreign policy councils. Its success led directly to a series of massive preemptive raids into Angola, bearing code-names like Super, Daisy, and Sceptic.[9] In this way, and in others, the Namibian conflict adds to the authoritative role of the SADF in foreign policy.

In effect, vast regions of Namibia are "governed" by the SADF, and the SADF claims a virtual veto over any settlement proposal. There is some evidence that the SADF sought to sabotage the 1982–83 Cape Verde Islands talks between DFAI and Angola. Even after Pik Botha returned with agreements for a preliminary package that included South African military withdrawal, military voices in the SSC rebuked him. In addition, top SADF brass often participate directly in the negotiation process. Maj. Gen. Charles Lloyd (chief of the SWATF until 1983), his successor, and Lt. Gen. Jannie Geldenhuys (chief of the army), and Gen. A.J. van Deventer (SSC) have been members of various negotiation delegations. MIS also participates, including its head, Gen. P.W. van der Westhuizen and Brigadiers van Tonder and Thirion. Although they appear to stand for subtly different orientations (for example, Lloyd and MIS the hawks and Geldenhuys the dove), they do bring a common professional military perspective to the proceedings. Members of government and those close to government profess that government wants a settlement on Namibia, but a quick agreement involving major South African concessions is not likely. Those in position to shape the outcome in Namibia, the military men, appear to favor the view that the Republic can best be defended from forward positions. When Gen. Constand Viljoen talks of pushing SWAPO forces as far back as possible, he evidently is alluding to spatial and territorial considerations.[10] Although Viljoen dutifully stresses that it is for government, not the SADF, to decide, he insists that South Africa should not "rush into a settlement." "We are capable of maintaining the military situation for a long time," Viljoen has stated. The government should, he continued, take the time to reach a long-lasting solution. Hidden in his imprecise words is a hard-line view that the military still has an indispensable role to play in Namibia, strategically and politically, and that SADF thinkers are extremely skeptical of any concessions to other parties in the negotiations. It is apparent that the military believes that it has stabilized the war zone.

The military may be upbeat about the war in Namibia, but the cost factors are getting out of hand. According to provisional figures, the "cost" of killing each SWAPO insurgent killed in 1984 was over R1.7 million.[11] Officially 584 SWAPO were killed in 1984 against South Africa's total subsidy of over R1 billion. If only the military costs, estimated at R547.5 million, are factored in, the cost for each insurgent killed would work out to R937,500. Although there were only 21 "contacts" a month between SWAPO and the security forces—a relatively low-intensity war—it and the military occupation are draining the South African treasury. The Botha government is being pushed toward settlement, despite the optimism of the SADF and its policy preferences.

So there is a division of perspectives between the military, which thinks it can "win," and the government, which wants to "win," but knows that the war can also smolder indecisively for years. SADF leaders are portentously signalling the politicians that they had better not do anything impetuous or irresolute. Viljoen has implied that even should a negotiated solution be reached, if it fails to meet the SADF's demands, the SADF might have "to go back in" when Namibia was "again burning." From this vantage, the SADF would seem to want to delay, as much as practical, a settlement that might lead to a SWAPO government in Windhoek. Independence for its own sake doesn't necessarily bring peace. Look at Angola, Mozambique, and Zimbabwe, Viljoen has pointed out. Just as importantly, the SADF is in an immediate position to engage in cross-border strikes, to undermine a cease-fire should an agreement be reached, or to submarine the transitional process to independence. Leverage, it would seem, still lies with Defence Headquarters, less so with DFAI.

III. DESTABILIZATION FOR A PURPOSE

It has been said of the SADF that it has no policy to pull together its tactics, that a series of strikes to destabilize neighboring governments do not constitute a larger design. By and large this is an unfair criticism. Certainly strategic thinkers in the SADF and people in the secretariat of the SSC have devoted great energy to devising a winning strategy for South Africa. One might dispute the wisdom of their strategy, the intelligence on which it depends, or their lack of sensitivity to black peoples' aspirations in South Africa and in the region, but one cannot in fairness to security specialists deny that they have tried to look at the big picture.

Sympathetic analysts might, in a form of ex post facto reasoning, seek to convince outsiders that the current success of Pretoria's peace offensive is tangible proof that a consistent policy of firmness (less generous analysts call it destabilization) has contributed directly to better relations in the region. It has, in other words, been destabilization with a purpose.

One cannot document with assurance a particular decision by government or agencies thereof to destabilize states in the region. Rather, one can arrive at such an assertion by assessing the sum total of a number of policy decisions and their cumulative impact on regional affairs. Although governmental rhetoric fastens on a desire for peaceful coexistence, constellation, and nonintervention as hallmarks of South African regional policy, actual policy consists of an extensive dossier of reports of large- and small-scale open and clandestine raids into nearby states, the effects of which have been to heighten insecurities in areas near the international borders with the Republic.[12] At first glance it may appear to be a series of unrelated, ad hoc responses to diverse stimuli. But in the aggregate what emerges is an unmistakable pattern of intimidation and coercion of governments already inclined to be hostile to Pretoria, insecure and even skittish about incursions from the last white regime in Africa.[13]

It is pointless to detail the various operations, charges, and denials in order to arrive at an empirical statement about conscious policy. Suffice to say that the list is long and damning. In volume, destabilizing activity probably reached its peak in late 1982 and early 1983. SADF forces on numerous occasions have struck into Angola, not just in hot pursuit but in large-scale, meticulously planned, coded operations that could only have been launched with the approval of government at the highest levels. Moreover, SADF forces have occupied vast stretches of Angolan territory for considerable periods of time, ostensibly to destroy and disperse large SWAPO concentrations of fighters and materiel, but also to bolster UNITA, to terrorize Namibian refugees and local Angolan peoples, and to demolish the economic infrastructure of the region nearest the border with Namibia.[14] Denial cannot undo the destruction which has been going on since 1975–76 and most actively pursued between 1980 and 1983. The agreements with Mozambique and Angola and the announcement of the nonaggression pact with Swaziland in 1984 seemed to signal an end to direct SADF strikes. It did not, apparently, terminate support for proxy organizations such as the MNR, UNITA, and the LLA.

It is necessary to outline the extent of the destabilization policy in order to examine the intentions of the security establishment. The military actions against Angola, ostensibly to negate preemptively the SWAPO incursions, have been described. South Africa's Angolan policy is an extension of its Namibian policy. Once Pretoria realized the promise of a military line, it followed that being able to manipulate domestic Angolan affairs, especially to bring about a UNITA role in government and a diminished role if not an end to Cuban presence, was not only desirable but within its grasp. SWAPO infiltrations from Angola were never denied, in fact Angola provided SWAPO's military arm, PLAN, with bases and training facilities. The rationale for cross-border strikes was in place. ANC activities in Mozambique, Lesotho, and Zimbabwe, by no means as extensive or open, nonetheless were undeniable. Once embarked on a course of aggressive defense, the case for South African military operations elsewhere in the region became easier.

The *Mozambique* file is full. It involves direct SADF action and support for a proxy movement hostile to the Frelimo government.[15] Most celebrated have been the major SADF cross-border commando raids against alleged ANC offices near Maputo. The first, in January 1981, was aimed at ANC operatives in Matola. It left thirty-one dead and many others wounded. Not as surgical and efficient as the SADF would have liked, this raid served as a signal to Mozambique that the policy of South African reticence to use its own force directly—a policy that had prevailed since Mozambique gained independence—no longer applied.

There have been several raids since then, including an air strike on the suburbs of Maputo in May 1983 in retaliation for the ANC car bomb attack outside the air force headquarters in Pretoria, and another commando raid in October 1983 against "an ANC target" in Maputo, officially in response to the ANC bombing in Warmbaths (Transvaal). These punishments are more symbolic than destabilizing. They illustrate South Africa's determination to take violent measures to defeat the ANC, and Mozambique's complete inability to defend either ANC facilities or its own territory.

By far more damaging to Mozambique has been South Africa's sponsorship of the MNR. Sanctuary, arms, supplies, training, and logistical support have been provided. And it is widely believed that the MNR radio station, the Voice of Free Africa, operated from South Africa. The MNR has proven to be most destructive. The economy, especially food distribution, has been disrupted. Sabotage is widespread, and in many areas of the country goods must be transported by armed convoy. Even on the verge of reaching agreement with Mozambique to refrain from interfering in internal affairs and not to allow its territory to be used by any group for purposes of committing acts of violence, terrorism or aggression against Mozambique, the South Africans denied that they assisted MNR. Mountains of evidence to the contrary exist.

Apparently the major reason South Africa supported the MNR was to pressure Mozambique to control, or better, to expel the ANC from its territory. Although there were no ANC military bases in Mozambique, most ANC operatives in South Africa got into the country by way of Mozambique and Swaziland. South Africa was not satisfied with Maputo's professions of innocence in assisting the ANC militarily. Pretoria wanted the ANC out.

For this reason the Mozambique government approached the South Africans at least three times before the final phase of negotiations leading to Nkomati. In private meetings with Pik Botha they tried to reach an agreement akin to a nonaggression pact. South Africa did not lessen its pressure until it was absolutely convinced that Maputo was prepared to put the stopper to ANC movements within its territory.

By contrast, however, the MNR continues to bedevil the Machel government. MNR claims some 10,000 fighters, and it operates in all but two of Mozambique's provinces. Unless the government can deliver economically and fast, the MNR is poised to exploit the disenchantment.

Not that the MNR is popular; far from it. Many MNR leaders are still identified with the Portuguese secret police and with South Africa. Rather it is that the Machel government is so vulnerable. Mozambicans want peace and food, and their government is in the dock. Maputo was driven to the treaty of nonaggression and the October 1984 cease-fire agreement with the MNR out of fear and hope. So far, although Maputo has taken steps effectively to nullify the ANC, there is little evidence that South Africa has done the same regarding MNR.[16]

Although South African officials seem intent on bringing the MNR and the Frelimo government to agree to end the fighting, the MNR seems increasingly able to operate beyond Pretoria's control. Funds and supplies are thought to be reaching MNR through the Comores Islands, Tanzania, and Malawi, from sources in Portugal, Germany, the Middle East, elsewhere in Africa, and possibly still from private and public groups in South Africa. Foreign Minister Pik Botha has devoted much energy to trying to persuade various suspected governments to end their assistance to the MNR, but the fighting intensifies. Hence, Mozambique is "not satisfied" with the alleged security benefits flowing from the Nkomati accord. Efforts by Pretoria to close the border to likely MNR suppliers have not served to reduce MNR military activities markedly, if at all. Political pressure is mounting, especially from the Mozambique army which never had been pleased with the Nkomati agreements, to abrogate the accord and to seek military assistance from the eastern bloc countries.

Lesotho has proven nearly as beset with problems as—and even more militarily exposed than—Mozambique. Lesotho is entirely surrounded by the Republic of South Africa and Transkei. Lesotho claims large stretches of the Orange Free State and is economically dependent on South Africa. On first achieving independence from Great Britain, Chief Jonathan Leabua pursued an accommodationist policy with South Africa, and many of the more militant nationalists in Africa accused him of serving as Pretoria's agent. For those leanings Lesotho was denied a role in the Front-Line States entente. Lesotho's commitment to black nationalism and against apartheid were suspect. More recently, however, Pretoria and Maseru have been on a collision course.

On the surface the issue is Lesotho's friendliness toward the ANC. Pretoria is determined to squeeze Lesotho into submission. The South Africans ideally want four things from Lesotho: a stoppage of anti-South African rhetoric; recognition of the Transkei and Ciskei; the expulsion of ANC elements and exiles from Lesotho; and an end to Lesotho's warming relations with the Soviet Union and other socialist bloc governments.

A variety of nonmilitary pressures have been employed. Arms shipped to Lesotho were impounded for several months at Durban. Presumably their passage can be halted under terms of Article 16 of the Customs

Union Agreement (between South Africa, Botswana, Lesotho, and Swaziland), which allows South Africa to prohibit certain imports "in the interests of security."[17] Basutos seeking work in South Africa are being refused admission to South Africa by sporadic border closings. The on-again-off-again Highlands water project has been subject to South African delays and threats to withdraw financial support.

More direct action took the form of a major SADF attack on Maseru. In a night raid in December 1982, forty-two "ANC terrorists" and civilians were murdered. Lesotho forces mounted virtually no resistance. This assault is openly acknowledged by the SADF. In September 1983, Lesotho eventually agreed to South Africa's demand that it expel some twenty-two refugees with ANC connections, but no direct link between the two events is apparent.

More persistent and potentially unsettling to the Jonathan government is the prospect of dealing with a South African-assisted Lesotho Liberation Army. Ntsu Mokhehle, leader of the Basutoland Congress Party (BCP), reportedly lives in South Africa. The BCP has been waging political war on Jonathan's Basutoland National Party (BNP) since before independence, and the BNP has sought to stifle the BCP. In 1979 the BCP founded the LLA, and South Africa has closed its eyes to the LLA operations from South African territory. Indeed, South African actions on behalf of the LLA may be even more positive. The BCP continues to be popular throughout Lesotho and among Basuto laborers in South Africa. Lesotho accuses South Africa of active encouragement and support for the LLA. The LLA operates out of the Orange Free State, QwaQwa, and Transkei. By using Transkei as a base of operations for the LLA, South Africa can force Lesotho to negotiate with Transkei, thereby evolving a form of de facto recognition. Two captured LLA members claimed to have been trained by a Major Mackenzie, a former Selous Scout (and an American) now with the Transkeian Defence Force. Pretoria repeatedly denies Lesotho's allegations about Pretoria's assistance to the LLA, but in 1984 a meeting between South African authorities and Lesotho dissidents was announced.[18] Earlier the two governments nearly had arrived at an agreement. In mid-1983 the foreign ministries of Lesotho and South Africa told the press in Johannesburg that the two states had agreed to stop "any subversive elements" from attacking each other. This might have been an informal precedent for the Nkomati Accord of 1984. But a follow-up meeting in Bloemfontein in late June ended in failure. Three days later LLA launched its heaviest offensive, and Pretoria introduced border curbs in July. More recently Pretoria appears to have abandoned Mokhehle in favor of a group of dissident politicians who head a new party, the Basuto Democratic Alliance. It is less openly violent, although support for factions of the LLA remain.

There are still some 11,000 South African refugees who fled into Lesotho and who, in the eyes of South African security forces, constitute a threat to the South African regime. But this is hardly a threat to South Africa. The ANC in Lesotho is and has been too weak to mount more than token resistance to Pretoria. Nonetheless, South Africa has unleashed its own refugee movement, the LLA, and its sabotage, assassination, and all-around harassment of Lesotho officials are an immediate threat to Jonathan, never the most popular of Africa's rulers. The disunity of the LLA itself accentuates the level of anti-Jonathan violence as each faction seeks to demonstrate to followers and outsiders its efficacy as leader of the most viable nationalist movement.

Coercive actions against *Zimbabwe* are most difficult to document.[19] South Africa believes that Prime Minister Robert Mugabe has honored his preindependence pledge not to assist the ANC. Nevertheless, South Africa's security specialists have sought, by means of propaganda, assassinations, economic pressures, coercive activities, and dirty tricks, to weaken the Mugabe government and the ANC in Zimbabwe. "Radio Truth" came on the air in March 1983 from South African territory. Its broadcasts in English, Shona, and Ndebele are hostile to Mugabe and Zimbabwe's brand of socialism. When Joe Gqabi, ANC representative to Zimbabwe, was shot outside his house in 1981, Zimbabwe police arrested his South African secretary and held her three weeks for questioning. She was forced to divulge details of ANC operations. A few months later the mystery of her strange treatment emerged when the white detective inspector in charge of her interrogation defected to South Africa and with him went the secretary's account of ANC operations.

Zimbabwean security officials say they believe that a number of former Rhodesians now in South Africa have been involved in the sabotage attacks (including the destruction of a large portion of Zimbabwe's military air craft in 1982). For example, Edward Sutton-Pryce, an ex-British military officer and deputy to Ian D. Smith, is employed at SADF headquarters in Pretoria. Emigrés are also alleged to be involved in recruiting and training black and white Zimbabweans, especially Ndebele from the southwest, into military units that could be employed against the central government. In addition, Mugabe has made repeated reference to a secret army, based in South Africa and allegedly being organized for Bishop Abel Muzorewa. South Africa denies that it allows any dissidents to train on its soil, but armed soldiers captured and killed in Zimbabwe confess to or can be shown to be Zimbabweans in exile with training experience in South Africa.

There was also an incident in August 1982, when three South African white soldiers were killed inside Zimbabwe. They were formerly Rhodesian soldiers. According to General Viljoen, they, along with fourteen black soldiers, had been on an "unauthorized mission" to free anti-Mugabe political prisoners held in a camp in southeast Zimbabwe.[20] Even if one challenges this story, and Zimbabwean authorities do, this leads one to speculate further on how many undetected "unauthorized missions" there have been into Zimbabwe and on why the SADF command was unable to account for seventeen men, to control them, and to prevent such an embarrassing episode.

In June 1984, Zimbabwe security officials offered detailed evidence supporting their charges that South Africa had been instrumental in supporting rebels operating in southern Matabeleland. Now Harare admits that Pretoria has temporarily halted its supplies in response to a series of unpublicized meetings between the two countries' security officials. There have been no confirmed reports of rebel infiltrations from South Africa since February 1984.

In *Swaziland*, where Pretoria's relations are generally good, it is believed that South African agents have engaged in secret raids, kidnappings, and assassinations of ANC members. Despite Mbabane's and Pretoria's determination to shut off the flow of ANC saboteurs into South Africa, Swaziland still was the principal conduit into Natal and the Transvaal. The fact is that Swaziland is not a serious target for South Africa's destabilization.

Botswana, by no means as close to Pretoria as is Swaziland, has also pledged to prevent ANC infiltration through its territory into South Africa. Botswana has, in fact, had more difficulty with the Zimbabwean forces violating its borders than with the SADF or SAP in recent years. This apparent immunity ended in June 1985, when the SADF, acting on intelligence supplied by the Security Police, destroyed an alleged ANC "nerve center" in Gaberone. With virtually no resistance from the Botswana Defence Forces, the South Africans attacked ten buildings scattered about the city, and killed at least twelve and wounded six.

Further afield, controversy has surrounded the extent of official SADF and MIS involvement in the aborted coup attempt in the *Seychelles*. Ex-SADF and ex-NIS personnel participated, and in their defense they have tried to implicate high officers of the SADF, MIS, and the South African government. It was later disclosed that some of the participants are still employed by the SADF.[21] The full story did not emerge from the Pietermaritzburg trial of the airplane hijackers or from the captured mercenaries first held in the Seychelles and later released. In fact, the South African authorities have sought to draw a curtain of silence, insofar as the law allows, over these issues. The minister of defense secured a clamp on evidence at the trial by invoking the General Law Amendment Act of 1969, section 29 of which provides that no person can be forced to give information if a minister of state signs an affidavit saying that the release of information would affect the security of state.[22] Later in 1982 police confiscated reporters' notebooks and documents about NIS links to Martin Dolinchek, who had been awaiting trial in the Seychelles on treason charges for his role in the coup attempt. A complaint from the director general of NIS invoked the Official Secrets Act. Evidence clearly showed that somebody in the SADF took a sympathetic view of the attempt, and it appeared to some of the accused that the imprimatur of SADF approval was put on the arrangements. SADF weapons were somehow made available to the mercenaries involved. Perhaps what is most disturbing is that SADF officers could act without the knowledge or approval of government or of their military superiors. Either the SADF staged the operation or else it was not an official SADF enterprise, in which case the SADF was negligent in not controlling its own personnel. To prevent further disclosures, the SADF declines to answer questions. "I do, however," said the minister of defense, "deem it in the interest of the persons concerned and for security considerations, also not in the public interest to disclose [further] information."[23]

Persistent accusations and reports of border incursions, military overflight violations, and even short-term territorial occupation against the territorial integrity of Angola, Mozambique, Lesotho, Botswana, Zambia, and Zimbabwe by South African military units, raids not always aimed at opponents of South Africa harbored in that state, constitute a pattern of intimidation and hostility, if not aggression, that is difficult to deny. If these were not enough, one might add unproven accusations of assassination attempts (the ANC alleges eighteen assassinations by South African agents outside of South Africa since 1974), sabotage, and intelligence "dirty tricks," and the destabilizing activities of counterrevolutionary movements targeting leftist and even some moderate black governments in the region. The evidence of South Africa's encouragement, sanctuary, training, equipping, financing, logistical, and diplomatic support contributes to a widespread atmosphere of animosity in the region. In some respects it is a mirror image of Soviet policy in southern Africa. That is because both South Africa and the Soviet Union share a similar policy style for opposite ends: they work through proxies to destabilize the region so as to bring regional governments to a sense of desperation that forces them to cooperate for an imposed order. After all, an opponent's weakness is one's own strength.

Resort to such activities demonstrates the extent of Pretoria's diplomatic and political insecurity. In fact, it is unwise to view diplomatic and military initiatives separately. They are very much integral parts of a single policy thrust. It so happens that the dominant thrust of policy since 1978 or so has been coercive. Policy by coercion and proxy is a measure of a pariah state caught in a deteriorating regional political balance.[24] It is true, as

General Malan has stated, that "South Africa has not yet used its iron fist" to the extent it might.[25] For South Africa the military trump card is a deceptive indicator of policy—superficially it reflects confidence, strength, and purpose, but in reality it may indicate desperation. It would seem, however, that the weakness and vulnerability of South Africa's neighbors, especially regarding food supply (thanks to the drought and to mismanagement), econommic incompetence and corruption, and military weakness, have driven them to collaborate with South Africa or acquiesce in the maintenance of the status quo.

Now that the Republic has secured agreements with governments to end their assistance to South Africa's black revolutionaries, Pretoria has embarked on a policy of restabilization. Nonaggression pacts or the promises of them are followed by the prospects for improved trade and infrastructural relations, customs rewards, and other forms of cooperation. A major agreement on the Cahora Bassa hydroelectric project was signed in May 1984 between South Africa, Mozambique, and Portugal. This came less than two months after the Nkomati Accord. The announcement of a nonaggression pact with Swaziland signed two years earlier was designed to add to the momentum created early in 1984. Some observers think that South Africa is using the promise of a revamped Customs Union Agreement as the inducement to pressure Lesotho and Botswana into signing formal nonaggression agreements. In short, the move from a foreign policy based principally on force to one employing largely economic instruments (with force conspicuously in the background and still employed by proxy movements in Mozambique and Angola) appears to indicate that "total national strategy" is well coordinated under P.W. Botha.

IV. THE EVOLVING DOCTRINE OF PREEMPTIVE INTERVENTION

The very success of the South African policies leading to a regional Pax Pretoriana has led South African policymakers to see the merits of a policy based on strength and coercion. South Africa has come to accede to the disruptive doctrine of regional preemptive intervention. Increasingly the government found it useful to employ or to encourage dissident factions from neighboring states to intervene against their home governments. Policy by proxy is not particularly unusual. What is distinctive is the extent of such activity, the care that South Africa has taken to develop these military forces, and the abject vulnerability of most of the target regimes. Since the rules of international law apply chiefly through the intermediary of the state, there appears to be little to inhibit the use of such forces against former homelands whose sovereignty and independence is universally questioned. Since no government but South Africa's recognizes such homeland governments, South Africa might directly intervene even without an "invitation" to do so, and then argue that no sovereignty is violated since no one recognizes homeland sovereignty. Without sovereignty the doctrine of nonintervention falls away. This is the virtue, if there is one, of a Brezhnev-like doctrine predicated on the concept of limited sovereignty.

But even direct intervention might be risky in terms of international disapprobation. Might Pretoria use Xhosas hostile to the Ciskeian government to subvert that government when it becomes increasingly uncontrollable from Pretoria or so weak as to represent a potential threat to the Republic? South Africa already has ethnic companies at the ready in the SADF. The rules of international law might be hard to apply in the cases of such shadowy statehood.

When it comes to intervention further afield one might attempt to justify intervention as the exercise of the traditional right of self-defense.[26] Alternatively, it might be rationalized as a form of counterintervention— that is, intervention to redress a balance of force that has been disrupted by another's outside intervention. In this case, the incursions into Angola might so qualify, but only in a contorted fashion, since the Cubans have the blessing, indeed, have been invited by the Luanda government. Nonetheless, the Cuban "threat" serves as a standing alibi for Pretoria, enabling it to vindicate South Africa's refusal to come to terms with the MPLA or with SWAPO or to abandon UNITA. Moreover, the Soviet/ Cuban involvement helps to guarantee against hostile pressure from the West, and especially the United States. The presence of socialist bloc forces is trumpetted as testimony that South Africa's struggle with the ANC and SWAPO is part of a global resistance to Soviet expansion and communist revolution. Ironic it is that Pretoria counters the Marxist menace by contributing to a continued Soviet/Cuban presence in Angola. Pretoria needs the Marxists from abroad to discredit its own indigenous revolutionaries.

The doctrine of hot pursuit, well established in international law, might on occasion be helpful, too. But South Africa would be hard-pressed to adopt that line in most of these cases, since the cross-border code-named operations are hardly in direct hot pursuit. Rather, they necessitate considerable planning and logistical support. Some take the form of explicitly punitive raids in retaliation against earlier strikes by revolutionary forces believed to be harbored in a neighboring state. What is more, even in legitimate cases of hot pursuit, how deep and for how long may the pursuer penetrate after contact has been broken off before the rationalization of "hot pursuit" no longer applies?

There is emerging in the world a doctrine of preemptive intervention based rather on the arrogance of relative power. Usually the objectives have been limited and precise. Preemptive intervention is exemplified by Israel into Lebanon and Iraq, Rhodesia into Zambia and Mozambique, the Soviet Union into Afghanistan, the U.S. strikes into Granada, Cambodia, and Laos, and the Vietnamese bombings in Cambodia. This is a form of anticipatory defense that, depending on the context and situation, may be more or less justifiable.

Sometimes intervention involves direct state acts (although usually covert); more often it employs proxies indigenous to the target state. According to this emerging political doctrine of preemptive intervention, the inherent right of self-help or self-defense warrants the use of preemptive intervention if: (1) a neighboring government is hostile to the intervening regime; (2) if it is not especially hostile nor directly abetting those exiles in arms against the intervening state but is unwilling or unable to curb their activities; or even more minimally (3) if it may at some future time either aid or be unable to control announced enemies of the intervening regime. This is by no means a widely accepted doctrine of law—indeed, few if any governments would publicly acknowledge their adherence to this norm. Rather it arises because in fact it is practiced by a number of states. A government may presumably do what its leaders perceive it must do to survive, sweepingly defined. It is argued that the security of the intervening state is jeopardized if it fails to act. If it is a case of state against state, it may be easier to rationalize than if forces of one state attack a nonstate party on the territory of a state granting sanctuary. The legal meaning of such acts is rather ambiguous. But insofar as unilateral acts of preemptive intervention have no collective basis, the determination of their legitimacy often rests with some international body, such as the Security Council or the General Assembly of the United Nations. In these instances, situational political criteria are generally applied. To the intervening government, legitimacy is usually not the crucial issue. A unilateral act of preemptive intervention derives its utility and what legitimacy it claims because the state's leaders perceive a condition of encirclement or embattlement. In their eyes it is unquestionably an act of self-defense.

Consider this as the international analogue to what in American constitutional law is known as the "bad tendency test," whereby government may limit in part one's constitutional first amendment right of free speech (in this case, a state's sovereignty) if there is a likelihood that such speech might at some future time lead to substantive evils that disrupt the good order of the state, thereby demonstrating a "bad tendency." Some elements in South African governing circles implicitly subscribe to such a view, international law and practice notwithstanding. The revolutionary socialist nature of some regimes, or their willingness to provide sanctuary for opponents of apartheid, or their instability per se, may be seen as hazardous in the long run, crying out for preventative action. Although Zimbabwe under Mugabe poses little threat to South African tranquility today, Mugabe would like to end apartheid if he could. Thus, it is not seen to be in South Africa's interest to have Mugabe or other Marxists consolidate their power in the region.

It is ironic that P.W. Botha would, at the same time that he subscribes to a hard-line foreign policy, try to push a liberalized (only in relative terms) line domestically. By approving uncritically the views and advise from his military thinkers, Botha may well be a prisoner of a narrow and incomplete reading of regional political realities. His views take on the quality of a self-fulfilling prophecy. There is something badly wrong, practically self-deluding, in the Defence view that appears to regard Zambia, for example, as a "Marxist satellite" in the same sense as Angola, Mozambique, and Zimbabwe.[27] Undeniably committed to Marxism though they are, one might also argue whether even these last three governments can fairly be called "satellites." Yet the recent series of meetings and agreements with socialist neighbors indicates that Defence doesn't always act on or even believe its own cant.

There is some evidence that P.W. does not entirely believe what he has been saying. The "peace offensive" of late 1983–84 presumably is predicated on the belief that the agreements will last, at least for a while. If these parties were indeed "satellites," agents of Soviet foreign policy, and if the Soviet Union is prepared to use all means at its disposal to destroy Pretoria, what confidence can be placed in these pacts? Certainly, Botha must perceive that these governments are capable and willing to act on their own interests, not just on Moscow's bidding. The military instrument has been used to great effect. It appears that this record of intervention, destabilization, and assistance to dissident movements was part of a larger effort to drive neighboring governments to the bargaining table. By this expedient, such states could be defanged, as it were, and brought into South Africa's larger defense scheme. These governments are thereby compromised, and the ANC and SWAPO politicians and forces left dangling. Unwittingly, Mozambique, Angola, Zimbabwe, and Zambia have become part of South Africa's defense perimeter, thereby formalizing what they have been averse to admit—that they are unable to contribute greatly to changing the apartheid system at the same time that they grapple with the extensive problems of statehood, nationhood, and economic survival.

In the past, senior military decision makers have been incapable of interpreting the intentions of their counterparts abroad. What South

Africa lacks, as U.S. Assistant Secretary of State Chester Crocker has written, is "the capacity for sophisticated threat assessment and political analysis,"[28] particularly regarding politics in black African states. This includes everything from their inability to appreciate the popularity of Robert Mugabe to their misunderstanding of U. S. politics in their initial invasion of Angola in 1975. American executive branch officials, no matter how highly placed, simply were not in a position to commit the government (and certainly not Congress) to assist in military operations abroad. Had South African officials really understood American politics, they would have realized this from the start.

As a result, the DFAI had been forced to conduct a responsive foreign policy, extinguishing brush fires of rage, incredulity, and criticism brought on by frequent SADF and badly disguised proxy thrusts at South Africa's neighbors, But DFAI persistence, and a confluence of fortuitous circumstances for the region, have driven black southern African governments to seek accommodation with South Africa. Neither side must be deluded into seeing these pacts as anything more than a temporary break from a fundamentally hostile conflict of interests. As John de St. Jorre has written, America is not a "mover and shaker" in southern Africa; it is a broker. "Mover and shaker" is an appellation that "sits firmly on the shoulders of South Africa, whose ruthless military, political and economic pressures on its black neighbors pressures which brought them first to their knees and then to the negotiating table." It is, in a nutshell, a "Pax Pretoriana."[29] "This is our region," said Pik Botha proprietarily.[30] But Pik Botha has also said that "it is raining peace in southern Africa."[31] Whether this was intended to be a conscious refutation of Andre Brink's message in *Rumours of Rain* is not clear.[32] But it seems that the Brink metaphor still applies— that when it finally rains, when the political drought for blacks is finally broken, the ensuing flood will wash all away with it. The peace that Botha celebrates is a fragile peace, at best. The ANC is not going to surrender because it has been forced to move its operations further from the target.[33] Governments forced to humble themselves and to sue for peace are not about to forget their humiliation. In the future, the Soviet bloc may be prepared again to keep the pot aboil. As long as apartheid lives, anti-apartheid lives. The present semblance of rapprochement is not yet the substance of a lasting rapprochement. Internal contradictions that have long tormented the region run too deeply to dissipate at the first exposure to pressure. South Africa would do well not to become mesmerized by its own military might and assertiveness.

CHAPTER VII:

Conclusions

South Africa's security establishment enjoys a greatly enhanced role in policymaking. It should not be assumed that this tendency toward the paramountcy of security is unique to South Africa. Throughout the third world and in both the United States and the Soviet Union indications are that a wide range of policy formerly involving civilian politicians almost exclusively is now subject to military initiative and approval. Supervision for the Granada invasion was turned over to military advisors once the President had given the go-ahead.[1] In the USSR problems and insecurities of succession among top Party leaders have also inflated the military's political role.

In South Africa there are essentially three types of explanations for this phenomenon. One is based on the situation, another is idiosyncratic, and a third is structural. The situational or systemic explanation emphasizes the military threat, isolation, and regional unrest facing South Africa. As a result there is a commitment to resist the "total onslaught" by mounting a "total national strategy." Gore Vidal once wrote: "In any given moment in a society's life, there are certain hot buttons that a politician can push in order to get a predictably hot response."[2] Building up the armed forces and deferring to military judgment was a predictable anodyne response to the hot button of "total onslaught." It was justified by many as a survival response in a militantly hostile world. Early in the regime of P.W. Botha it became manifest that the defense elite had achieved greater status and power, especially in comparison to its place in the Vorster scheme.

A situational analysis requires, as well, that the power shifts described in these pages not be divorced from their domestic political context. And this, in turn, can be based on idiosyncratic factors. P.W. Botha is determined to lead South Africa through its present malaise. His governmental experience lies with the defense forces, which he has come to admire and respect. One journalist exaggeratedly wrote that the governmental setup was "popularly known as 'General Botha's Junta,' " a term, it might be added, that I never otherwise encountered when doing research on the phenomenon.[3] Surely it is an overstatement to say, as did one official of the DFAI, that "the day of the generals is at hand." Botha's would appear to be a sort of De Gaulle stratagem by which essential, yet manageable or controlled, change would be devised and implemented with the concurrent force of the state and its instruments of coercion. Government will be flexible and pragmatic in creating a domestic and foreign policy order, but unswervingly firm in dealing with real challenges to its stability and authority. The National Party loyalists and the rightwing of the Party are the ballast Botha must bear in order to instill flexibility into the South African system.

Which are the genuine threats to the system and who is to make that determination? How much change is necessary to defuse an embryonic revolutionary situation? It has been claimed, for example by Dr. John Seiler, that members of the SADF general staff sent a memorandum to P.W. Botha, after the Soweto uprising when he was still minister of defence, "implying that some form of military takeover might be necessary to bring about socio-political changes." Because in their view the Vorster regime was unable or unwilling to respond creatively to the Soweto challenges, SADF leadership felt that it was necessary to inform their civilian superior of their misgivings. Their memorandum merely confirmed P.W. Botha's predilections.[4] It is to be a changed order in which the essence of the system is to remain unchanged. Those who rule will continue to rule largely because they have discarded the excess ideological baggage of the past and because they have streamlined the governmental machinery and instruments of control as never before. Mr. Botha would seem to be building for the long haul, and with the approval of his military associates.

The top military brass are strikingly young. General Malan was forty-six when he took over as commanding officer of the SADF and fifty when he became minister of defense. General Viljoen was only forty-two when he assumed command of the Army, and Lt. Gen. Jack Dutton became chief of staff of the SADF at the age of forty-seven. There is, additionally, a certain homogeneity among the men who achieve high rank in the armed services. At the top, political reliability matters. Most of the senior officers rose to authority before P.W. became prime minister. It is now decreed that all who aspire to leadership earn a B. Mil. at the Military Academy at Saldanha Bay. A certain conformity of thought can be imposed upon degree candidates. In this fashion candidates for entry into the senior circle can be evaluated, and the less committed and critical can be sifted out.

In a way, one might perceive an "informal master plan" developing, and, characteristic of the military mind, although it may be *verligte*, it is still very committed to the continuation of the white dominant society.

There are, of course, personality differences and personal divisions among ambitious men. These might easily be translated into different policy preferences from time to time. It is difficult to think of the military as a pressure group in any formal sense. Although their homogeneity is assured, the divisions at the top between hard-liners who lean toward a law, order, and peace qua stability line and others who focus on the socio-economic dimensions of order—the Winning Hearts and Minds philosophy—are great. Moreover, political divisions in the country, especially among the Afrikaner volk, can heighten latent or potential factions within the military. Intraservice rivalry, competition between rank cohorts, and divisions within the officer corps based on socio-economic backgrounds are likely lines of cleavage. But compared to intra-armed forces competition elsewhere, these differences have proven to be marginal.

P.W. Botha was not content merely with bringing his own men, who happened to be mostly from the defense establishment, into key roles in government. He felt it necessary to reorganize and restructure the decisional process to enable South Africa to respond more effectively to the problems at hand, and to take preclusive steps to facilitate over-all policy goals. Indeed, the very definition of goals and strategies had, in the past, been left to chance or unsystematic declaration.

Yet the structures, once in place, become an element in the political mix, in their own right. This is most apparent in structures resisting changes that may threaten their power or existence. Even efflorescent institutions instinctively behave in ways designed to solidify or enhance their power. The security establishment is a model example. To be sure, social structures are determined by the character of the situation facing that society. William H. McNeill goes even further when he argues that the character of military technology and organization dominant in place and time is the paramount social determinant in that it outlines the paradigmatic structures to which society and the military must conform.[5]

Throughout this book I have discussed and documented this undeniable trend toward a greater reliance and involvement of the security establishment in decision making and policy output. The problem for the social scientist is all too evident. By setting out to study a particular phenomenon, one may inadvertently fasten on confirmatory data to the neglect of evidence or events that do not corroborate the basic hypothesis being examined.

In this respect it is vital to point out that the findings are not all one-sided. The "defense family," if it can be called that, does not always get its own way, and its influence is not uniformly high on all issues. Indeed, it is unclear which policies the "defense family" would prefer in every case. There is a deep-rooted Boer resistance to a standing professional army, and a reticence to give that force too much authority independent of the elected government. Such an outlook stems from the same colonial experience and mentality that led American colonists to press for constitional provisions that assured civilian supremacy over the military, the right of all citizens to bear arms (in order to form their own militia, congressional control over the budget, and protection against the quartering of soldiers in private houses without permission of the owners. The British colonial authorities, after all, made excessive demands on the American colonists. When the colonists opposed or threatened to revolt against what they regarded to be exploitative British policies, the authorities sought to impose their will on the recalcitrant colonists. That included the imposition of force involving both British and, occasionally, mercenary forces from the continent. This led eventually to the war for independence, and once having achieved independence, the Founding Fathers vowed to legitimize their opposition to parasitic armed forces.[6]

In its South African construct, the concept of a *volksleer* (people's army) is widely accepted. This norm has yet to be reconciled fully with a professionalized, career armed force. This Afrikaner apprehension is supplemented by the English-speakers' "liberal" leanings, distrustful of military incursions into the realm of civil affairs. Although it is highly respected, the SADF cannot do as it pleases in national politics. This wariness of military government or of the "creeping coup," whereby the forces insinuate themselves into a wide range of institutions and policies, is also accompanied by a deep respect and admiration for the military. In parliamentary debates a member may be critical of defense expenditures or of particular SADF policy, but he often backs off to claim that he did not intend to criticize the SADF itself or to denigrate the "wonderful work" they were doing for "all" of South Africa.

There are, as well, other individuals and institutions who also challenge P.W. Botha's reliance on the security establishment. In the Party and in the cabinet are powerful forces with slightly different agenda for government, or at least slightly different priorities. Although individual political fortunes shift regularly, it would appear that other leaders have been able to accumulate power. Some are not especially close to the security establishment, although unlike the DFAI they are not in direct competition with it either. For example, General Malan did not immediately assume a place of great importance in Party councils and in Parliament as some had expected when he was first named to cabinet.[7] Although his role has not been weakened since October 1980, it does appear that he has been subject to intensive scrutiny and on-the-job political and partisan training. General Malan is an outsider in NP politics. He may be popular nationally, but he has no provincial base in the Party. Party loyalists have long been reticent to reward coopted leaders too rapidly. Hence, individuals such as Pik Botha (diplomat), Dr. Gerrit Viljoen (educator), Dr. Owen Horwood (economist), and General Malan were expected to pay their partisan dues, so to speak, before gaining the topmost ranks in the NP. In the country, Malan, as head of the SADF, had almost been beatified. Once in cabinet, however, he was forced to descend from the meritocracy of the SADF's Olympia to the swampy backwater of politics and parliament. He was not at ease. A case might be made that the defense establishment had been better represented when P.W. Botha was minister of defense and General Malan served as chief of the SADF.

Likewise, elements in the cabinet responsible for the economic well-being of the country are wary of apportioning too many resources to the armed forces and are keenly aware of the disorder that arises from expanded national service and Citizen Force obligations for economically active men. Of course, other elements of the economic community, in government and in the private sector, argue that their efforts, especially at regional investment, trade and general economic cooperation, are made more burdensome by an aggressive military posture toward neighboring states. Economic instruments of foreign policy gain in effectiveness by a patient buildup of links and trusted relationships—they can be swiftly dissipated by threats and open or clandestine military strikes into states with which ostensibly correct relations are sought.

In another sense, although the SSC has been regarded as a sounding board for SADF views, in a way it might also become a check on the SADF. It is not automatic that the SSC's secretariat must be dominated by military or ex-military personnel. Likewise, although its composition is established by law, the relative weight given to particular voices can vary, especially as the prime minister, or presumably in the new dispensation the executive president, changes. The SSC is not a Chiefs of Staff meeting. It is very much a part of the civil government. Many of its members must answer to their constituencies, however they perceive them. The principle of political paramountcy in the decision-making process is still strong.

Since P.W. Botha became prime minister he has reorganized the executive branch. This involves a heavy emphasis on planning, administrative reorganization and coordination, and a far greater reliance on professional advice, even if they entail bypassing the normal state machinery. The SADF has made its considerable organizational skills available to Botha, and in the process has seen its role grow in power and stature. All aspects of government planning are now undertaken with strategy and security in mind. "Regional planning, economic planning, manpower planning, constitutional planning—the whole gamut is influenced by security and internal stability considerations."[8] Executive government demands decisive, efficient, and farsighted leadership. The managerial revolution in South Africa itself has been strengthened by the armed forces with its distinctive hierarchical leadership style. The military, in turn, benefits from a government that effectively accepts its framework of analysis and its strategic-ideological mind-set.

The military alone does not possess these skills and perspectives. And it alone does not have access to power brokers in government. P.W. Botha is open to ideas from all "acceptable" and knowledgeable quarters. This heightens governmental dependence on civil servants rather than on elected partisan officials of limited administrative experience. In the SSC, for example, there are some working groups empowered to take decisions on their own, thereby giving civil servants power unencumbered by the need to secure immediate political approval in Parliament.

Part of the explanation for the rise of the security establishment in central decision-making organs is that both P.W. Botha and his closest NP associates on the one hand, and the military-industrial axis on the other, appreciate the need for change in South Africa. The issue of po-litical-governmental reorganization is not an apolitical desire for efficiency or rationalization. It is very much tied to the leaders' tolerance and awareness of the need for reform, a controlled and modulated reform to be sure, that seeks better to defend the essence of the South African status quo. They debate the means constantly. It is a contest between those who insist on a military solution and those who prefer political or diplomatic solutions (coercion against persuasion—firepower against hearts and minds). They debate tactics and strategies. The question is not about ends. All at the top are committed to the maintenance of the class/race based system. In this regard the best form of conservatism is seen by some as a managed liberalism.

Magnus Malan and most high-ranking officers in the SADF believe that South Africa's future solutions must be principally political, but within the context of a secure and stable order. The military arm is therefore indispensable. But it is not employed in every case. Frequently, military leaders appreciate, perhaps more than some civilian politicians, the limits of military power. The Joint Chiefs of Staff in the United States reportedly unanimously opposed sending U.S. Marines to Lebanon in 1982.[9] But on many issues today, the military shares a perspective with key partisan leaders and hence their influence, based on shared values and analytical modes, flourishes.

The Republic of South Africa faces a state of "pre-semi-war," a situation that it has largely brought on itself. Consequently, the rise of the security establishment has been almost inevitable. The problem for the South African government is that it is faced with a virtually insoluble dilemma. It feels that it must alert the people to the threat posed by a total onslaught and must prepare itself for the expanding conflict, at the very same time that it must try to reassure the electorate that panic and desperate or extreme measures are not required. To reconcile these conflicting views may be asking too much of any government, least of all one whose popular base is, by choice and design, narrowly defined and exclusive.

GLOSSARY

ANC—African National Congress: the principal revolutionary black African party/ movement, banned since 1960 and currently committed to the violent overthrow of the South African regime.

Armscor—Armaments Development and Manufacturing Corporation: a state corporation created in 1968 to develop and manufacture armaments, and thereby negate the effects of the international arms embargo on South Africa.

BCP—Basutoland Congress Party: the chief opposition party in Lesotho.

BNP—Basutoland National Party: the ruling party in Lesotho and led by Chief Jonathan Leabua.

BOSS—Bureau for State Security: a once powerful intelligence and "dirty tricks" organization established in 1969 and, after being implicated in the information scandal, replaced by the Department of National Security, which in 1980 was renamed the National Intelligence Service.

CIO—Central Intelligence Organization: Rhodesian political and espionage network.

COIN—Counter-insurgency strategic emphasis and training undergone by segments of the SAP and SADF, in which the principal enemy is assumed to be civil, irregular, popular, and clandestine.

CONSAS—Constellation of Southern African States: a projected structure devised by Pretoria that unites regional states (including South Africa and the "independent" homelands) in an economic, functional, and possibly defensive organization.

CP—Conservative Party: a white opposition party to the right of the ruling National Party. Formed by dissident NP members in 1982.

CSIR—Council for Scientific and Industrial Research: the state agency charged with coordinating scientific reseach and with supporting and conducting same. Involved to some extent in defense-related research.

DFA—Department of Foreign Affairs: the executive department in charge of foreign policy. In 1980 amalgamated with the Department of Information to become DFAI

DFAI—Department of Foreign Affairs and Information.

DMLC—Defence Manpower Liaison Committee: a state-organized committee to facilitate communication between the SADF, private employers of white labor, and the Department of Manpower Utilization and Development.

DOD—Department of Defence.

DONS—Department of National Security. See BOSS.

FNLA—Frente Nacional de Libertação de Angola: a largely Bakongo movement opposing the MPLA government in Angola and operating from sanctuary in Zaire.

Frelimo—Frente de Libertação de Moçambique: the governing party in Mozambique since independence in 1975.

GBS—Gesamentlike Bestuursentrums: Joint Management Centres that coordinate security activities on a regional basis.

HNP—Herstigte Nasionale Party: a right-wing white opposition party that sometimes cooperates with the CP. Formed in 1969.

HSRC—Human Sciences Research Council: a state-sponsored social science research body that sometimes does its own, largely survey, research and sometimes contracts for research projects.

Iscor—South African Iron and Steel Industrial Corporation, Ltd.: a conglomerate parastatal firm created in 1928.

KEOSSA—Komitee vir Ekonomiese en Ontwikkelingsamewerking in Suider-Afrika (Committee for Economic and Development Cooperation in Southern Africa): an interdepartmental committee established in 1979 to advise government on developmental assistance for the ex-homelands and neighboring states.

LLA—Lesotho Liberation Army: established in 1979 by the BCP, the LLA is harbored in and assisted by South Africa, and occasionally raids Lesotho government targets across the border.

MIS—Military Intelligence Section: formerly the Military Intelligence but renamed in 1971. Now under the Directorate of Military Intelligence.

MNR—Mozambique National Resistance - see Renamo.

MPLA—Movimento Popular de Libertação de Angola: the ruling party in Angola since independence in 1975.

NIS—National Intelligence Service: since 1970 the successor of BOSS and DONS.

NP—National Party: South Africa's governing party since 1948.

NRP—New Republic Party: the successor to the United Party. Particularly strong among English-speakers in Natal.

OAU—Organization of African Unity: formed in 1963 as the regional organization of independent black states of Africa.

PAC—Pan-Africanist Congress: banned since 1960, this black nationalist movement has lost much of its support to the ANC.

PF—Permanent Force: the full-time career arm of the SADF.

PFP—Progressive Federal Party: the official opposition in the House of Assembly, to the left of the NP.

PLAN—Peoples Liberation Army of Namibia: the military wing of SWAPO.

Poqo—the now suppressed armed forces of the PAC.

Renamo—Resistência Nacional Moçambicana: also known as MNR, in violent opposition to Frelimo government, this group was set up by the Rhodesians and later sustained by South Africa.

RSA—Republic of South Africa.

SABC—South African Broadcasting Corporation: a public corporation with a legal monopoly on radio and TV transmissions.

SADF—South African Defence Force.

Safmarine—South African Marine Corporation, Ltd.: a parastatal corporation since 1946, this firm has over forty ships engaged in oceangoing shipping.

SAP—South African Police.

Sasol—South African Coal, Oil and Gas Corporation, Ltd.: created in 1950 by the South African government to produce gasoline and petrochemical by-products from coal and shale.

Soweto—South Western Townships: the major black "group area" near Johannesburg. Perhaps 15 to 2 million people reside there.

SSC—State Security Council: the paramount cabinet committee established by law in 1972 and responsible for advice and decisions involving security and defense in the broadest sense.

SWAPO—South West Africa People's Organization: the predominant voice for black nationalism in Namibia, it contains a domestic (legal) wing and an illegal revolutionary wing that operates in exile.

SWATF—South West African Territorial Force: military forces for the internal government of South West Africa, fundamentally controlled by SADF.

TDF—Transkei Defence Force.

TRC—Terrorism Research Centre: a private company doing research and providing advice to government and private bodies on questions of security. Based in Cape Town.

UDF—Union Defence Forces: South Africa's armed forces before the establishment of a Republic in 1961, after which the term SADF was applied.

UNISA—University of South Africa: a large, state-financed correspondence univerity based in Pretoria.

UNITA—União Nacional para a Independência Total de Angola: the major indigenous opponent to MPLA, based largely in southeast Angola and receiving extensive assistance from RSA. UNITA has widened its insurgency since 1979.

UP—United Party: the principal white centrist opposition party from 1948 until the 1977 elections and its dismemberment into PFP, NRP, and the South African Party.

WHAM—Winning hearts and minds: code words for a counterinsurgency policy that stresses psychological manipulation, political flexibility, and finesse rather than uncompromising coercion of the indigenous black population.

Notes

1. INTRODUCTION AND IDEOLOGICAL CONTEXT

1. *Sunday Times* (Johannesburg), 20 June 1982, p. 34.

2. *Sunday Express* (Johannesburg), 20 June 1982, p. 22.

3. For example, Chester A. Crocker, *South Africa's Defense Posture: Coping with Vulnerability* (Beverly Hills & London: Sage, 1981); Washington Papers, Vol. IX, p. 16. Crocker is currently U.S. assistant secretary of state for African affairs. Philip Frankel, "Race and Counter-Revolution: South Africa's 'Total Strategy,' " *Journal of Commonwealth and Comparative Politics*, XVIII, no. 3 (October 1980), p. 279; Ngqungqushe, "The National Security Doctrine," *Sechaba* (March 1982), pp. 20–23; H.L., "The National Security Doctrine," *Sechaba* (June 1982), pp. 20–28; and, "Reaching into Government," *Financial Mail* (Johannesburg), vol. 82, no. 2 (8 October 1982), pp. 143–45. Particularly since the publication of Deon Geldenhuys and Hennie Kotzé, "Aspects of Political Decision-Making in South Africa," *Politikon*, X, no. 1 (June 1983), pp. 33–45; Simon Jenkins, "Destabilisation in Southern Africa," *Economist*, vol. 288, no. 7298 (16 July 1983), pp. 19–28; and Kenneth W. Grundy, *The Rise of the South African Security Establishment: An Essay on the Changing Locus of State Power*. Bradlow Series No. 1 (Braamfontein: South African Institute of International Affairs, August 1983), The institute is hereinafter cited as SAIIA.

4. Republic of South Africa, Department of Defence (hereinafter cited as RSA, DOC), *White Paper on Defence and Armaments Supply, 1984* (Cape Town: Department of Defence, 1984), pp. 1–3.

5. Edwin S. Munger, *Notes on the Formation of South African Foreign Policy* (Pasadena: Grant Dahlstrom/The Castle Press, 1965), p. 85.

6. See Heribert Adam, "Perspectives on the Literature: Critical Evaluation," in *Ethnic Power Mobilized: Can South Africa Change?* Heribert Adam and Hermann Giliomee (New Haven: Yale University Press, 1979), pp. 16–60; and Harrison M. Wright, *The Burden of the Present: Liberal–Radical Controversy over Southern African History* (Cape Town: David Philip, 1977).

7. See, for example, André du Toit and Hermann Giliomee, *Afrikaner Political Thought: Analysis and Documents*, vol. I, 1790–1850 (Berkeley: University of California Press, 1983).

8. Ivor Wilkins and Hans Strydom, *The Super-Afrikaners: Inside the Afrikaner Broederbond* (Johannesburg: Jonathan Ball, 1978); and J.H.P. Serfontein, *Brotherhood of Power: An Exposé of the Secret Afrikaner Broederbond* (London: Collins, 1979).

9. See Kenneth W. Grundy, *Defense Legislation and Communal Politics: The Evolution of a White South African Nation as Reflected in the Controversy Over the Assignment of Armed Forces Abroad, 1912–1976*, Papers in International Studies, Africa Series No. 33, 1978 (Athens: Ohio University Center for International Studies, 1977); and R. Dale, "The South African Armed Forces and Their Link with the United Kingdom and the Commonwealth of Nations, 1910–1961," *Militaria*, IX, no. 1 (1979), pp. 1–11.

10. As quoted in Deon Geldenhuys, *Some Foreign Policy Implications of South Africa's "Total National Strategy," with particular reference to the* "12-point plan" (Braamfontein: SAIIA, March 1981), p. 3.

11. As quoted in the *Star* (Johannesburg), 10 September 1977. Unless otherwise noted, all references to the *Star* are from the weekly air edition. A more recent SADF statement on this issue is General C. L. Viljoen, "The Scourge of the Civilized World," *Paratus*, vol. 34, no. 8 (August 1983), pp. 22–23, 36.

12. RSA, DOD, *White Paper on Defence and Armaments Supply, 1982* (Cape Town: South African Navy Printing and Photographic Unit, 1982), p. 2.

13. RSA, House of Assembly, *Debates (Hansard)*, 31 January 1978, cols. 103–104. Hereinafter cited as: Assembly, *Debates*.

14. Ibid., col. 105.

15. Ibid., 21 February 1983, cols. 1425–29. Minister Louis LeGrange was referring to Lodge's presentation to the African Studies Association in Washington, D.C., "The African National Congress in South Africa, 1976–1982: Guerilla War and Armed Propaganda," (xerox copy); and to Trevor Jones in the *Star*, 31 December 1982.

16. *White Paper on Defence, 1984*, p. 2.

17. Deon Geldenhuys, *What Do We Think? A Survey of White Opinion on Foreign Policy Issues* (Braamfontein: SAIIA, November 1982), pp. 6–7; and *What Do We Think? A survey of White Opinion on Foreign Policy Issues—Number Two* (Braamfontein: SAIIA, September 1984), pp. 7–8.

18. For example, P. W. Botha in Assembly, *Debates*, 8 March 1979, col. 2067; and 21 March 1980, cols. 3317–19.

19. Ibid., 28 January 1981, cols. 235–36.

20. Jan A. DuPlessis, "Soviet Blueprint for Southern Africa," *Paratus*, vol. 34, no. 6 (June 1983), p. 13; and, *Paratus*, vol. 34, no. 5 (May 1983), pp. 20–21.

21. *Newsweek*, 21 March 1983, pp. 21, 18; and Harold J. Berman, "The Devil and Soviet Russia," *Newsweek*, 9 May 1983, p. 8. See also Reagan's speech to the British Parliament in June 1982, and the National Security Decision Directive 75.

22. Assembly, *Debates*, 28 January 1981, col. 236.

23. L.J. Boulle, *Constitutional Reform and The Apartheid State: Legitimacy, Consociationalism and Control in South Africa* (New York: St. Martin's Press, 1984).

24. See Deon Geldenhuys, *South Africa's Search for Security Since the Second World War* (Braamfontein: SAIIA, September, 1978); and Robert S. Jaster, *South Africa's Narrowing Security Options*, Adelphi Paper No. 159 (London: International Institute for Strategic Studies, 1980).

25. "How 'total' is the total onslaught?", *Paratus*, vol. 34, no. 7 (July 1983), p. 33.

26. Frankel, "Race and Counter-Revolution," p. 273.

27. First mention of a similar idea in South Africa, although applied to the white community and its military orientation and advocating the use of a commando structure as part of COIN activities and to resist a foreign invasion, appeared in: Neil Orpen, *Total Defence* (Cape Town: Nasionale Boekhandel, 1967). See also Anthony Harrigan, *Defence against Total Attack* (Cape Town: Nasionale Boekhandel, 1965), in which many of the ideas about total onslaught and total national strategy were advanced long before the terms became de rigueur in South African strategic circles. Harrigan is an American right-wing journalist. Philip H. Frankel in *Pretoria's Praetorians: Civil-Military Relations in South Africa* (Cambridge: Cambridge University Press, 1984), pp. 46–70, sees the roots of SADF thinking in the writings of French general and strategist Andre Beaufre, *An Introduction to Strategy (with Particular Reference to Problems of Defence, Politics, Economics and Diplomacy in the Nuclear Age* (London: Faber and Faber,

1963) and *Strategy of Action* (London: Faber and Faber, 1967). These two books, Frankel writes, are perhaps the most widely quoted in the curricula, syllabi, and seminar groups held at the South African Military Academy and the Joint Defence College. In addition he cites J.J. McCuen, *The Art of Counter-Revolutionary War: The Strategy of Counter-Insurgency* (London: Faber and Faber, 1966), and Robert Thompson, *Defeating Communist Insurgency* (London: Chatto and Windus, 1966) as prominent works shaping total strategy thinking.

2. THE GROWTH OF THE SECURITY FORCES AND THE EVOLUTION OF STRATEGIC PLANS

1. Budgetary data are published regularly. Force levels are more classified, although the International Institute for Strategic Studies in London annually provides fairly reliable estimates. Much has been pulled together in International Defence and Aid, *The Apartheid War Machine: The Strength and Deployment of the South African Armed Forces*. Fact Paper on Southern Africa No. 8 (London: IDAF, April 1980).

2. 1982–83 and 1983–84 cash budget figures by department are contained in *Financial Mail*, vol. 88, no.1 (1 April 1983). Estimated expenditures for 1985–86 are from *Africa Research Bulletin* (Econ. series), vol. 22, no. 3 (30 April 1985), p. 7684.

3. L.H Gann and Peter Duignan, *South Africa: War? Revolution? Peace?* (Cape Town: Tafelberg, 1979), pp.38–39.

4. See RSA, DOD, *White Paper on Defence, 1984*, p. 18.

5. As reported in Assembly, *Debates*, 3 April 1984, col. *4270*, during the debate on the Appropriation Bill.

6. In an explanatory memorandum to the Defence Estimates quoted in "Security: The True Cost of Peace," *Financial Mail*, vol. 89, no. 5 (29 July 1983), pp. 35–36. A systematic discussion of budgetary analysis as it applies to the SADF can be found in Philip A. Frankel, *Pretoria's Praetorians: Civil-Military Relations in South Africa* (Cambridge: Cambridge University Press, 1984), pp. 71–79.

7. "Security," *Financial Mail*, vol. 89, no. 5 (29 July 1983), pp. 35–36.

8. International Institute for Strategic Studies, *The Military Balance: 1983–1984* (London: IISS, 1984), p. 73. The IISS estimates may be a bit low. Deon Geldenhuys puts the October 1981 figures at 33,000 PF and 58,000 national servicemen. These figures were reported to him by the SADF itself. See *The Diplomacy of Isolation: South African Foreign Policy Making* (Johannesburg: Macmillan, 1984), p. 141.

9. *Star*, 19 February 1983, p. 2.

10. *Collier's* 1983 Year Book (New York: Macmillan, 1982), p. 299.

11. The larger manpower issues and the political debate between the SADF and the business community, especially over the 1982 law, are discussed in Frankel, *Pretoria's Praetorians*, pp. 142–47. See also "Extended Military Service: Why Is It Essential?" *Paratus*, vol. 33, no. 4 (April 1982), pp. 26–28.

12. Kenneth W. Grundy, *Soldiers Without Politics: Blacks in the South African Armed Forces* (Berkeley: University of California Press, 1983).

13. *Sunday Express*, 24 May 1981; and 30 May 1982; *Sunday Tribune* (Durban), 24 May 1981; *Rand Daily Mail* (Johannesburg), and *Star*, 29 May 1982 (daily edition).

14. "Army and Politics," part 3, *Sechaba* (June, 1980), p. 11.

15. For example, Martin Spring, "Base SA national service on this simple principle," *Star*, 10 June 1984, p. 2.

16. *White Paper on Defence, 1984,* p. 13.

17. Assembly, *Debates,* 17 February 1984, Q.cols. 241–43.

18. *Star,* 9 January 1984, p. 4.

19. Assembly, *Debates,* 17 February 1984, Q.cols. 241–43; 6 March 1984, Q.cols. 494–95.

20. Brig. C. C. van der Westhuizen quoted in the *Star,* 30 October 1982, p. 3. See also the excellent series on the defense situation by Andrew Walker in the *Star,* 1–5 June 1982 (daily edition).

21. Brig. van der Westhuizen in the *Star,* 30 October 1982, p. 3.

22. *Star,* 2 October 1982, p. 3; and Dr. W. J. Snyman in Assembly, *Debates,* 17 May 1984, col. 6812.

23. See Grundy, *Soldiers Without Politics,* pp. 118–33 et passim; and B. B. Goodall in Assembly, *Debates,* 17 May 1984, col. 6790.

24. *Star,* 1 June 1982, p. 12. Interestingly, in 1976 Major-General Neil Webster spoke of "at least another 10 years before there is a situation where we're not threatened."*Sunday Tribune,* 29 May 1976, pp. 1, 15.

25. Statutes of the Republic of South Africa, Defence Act of 1957, Sec. 3 (2)a. See also *Star,* 15 October 1984, p. 9.

26. Jonathan Kapstein, "Armed Confrontation Builds in South Africa," *Proceedings of the U.S. Naval Institute,* vol. 107, no. 12 (December 1981), pp. 37–38.

27. *Sunday Times,* 13 July 1976.

28. See the *Citizen* (Johannesburg), 23 April 1982 (Schwarz); Assembly, *Debates,* 17 April 1978, col. 4835 (Raw); *Rand Daily Mail,* 11 November 1978 (editorial); *Sunday Times,* 8 July 1979, p. 16 (editorial); and M. Hough, "Strategiese Aspekte van die Witskrif oor Verdediging en Krygstuigvoorsiening 1979," *ISSUP Strategiese Oorsig* (September 1979), p. 6.

29. Quoted in the *New York Times,* 7 September 1981.

30. *Rand Daily Mail,* 5 June 1982, p. 5.

31. *Los Angeles Times,* 18 March 1982, part I-C, p. 6; and *Star,* 5 January 1983. See also Lodge, " The ANC in South Africa."

32. "Changing defence strategy," *Financial Mail,* vol. 82, no. 3 (15 January 1982), pp. 190–91.

33. Ibid., p. 191.

34. *Star,* 13 July 1982 (daily edition), p. 19; and *Rand Daily Mail,* 13 July 1982, p. 1. See also Assembly, *Debates,* 7 June 1982, cols. 8411–8571; and 11 June 1982, cols. 9416–50; and especially Gen. Malan's explanation in " 'Total Mobilisation' Biggest Misconception," *Paratus.* vol. 33, no. 7 (July 1982), pp.34–35, 81.

35. *Financial Mail,* vol. 85, no. 4 (23 July 1982), p. 403.

36. "Kmdmt Noord-Transvaal in drie verdeel," *Paratus,* vol. 34, no. 10 (October 1983), p. 13.

37. *Star,* 19 October 1982, p. 4.

38. Statutes of the Republic of South Africa, Defence, National Key Points Act, no. 102, of 1980, pp. 971–77; or *Government Gazette,* vol. 181, no. 7134 (25 July 1980), pp. 3–9. See also: "Security," supplements to *Financial Mail,* vol. 89, no. 3 (15 July 1983), esp. pp. 54–56; and vol. 43. no. 7 (17 August 1984), esp. pp. 12–13.

39. *Rand Daily Mail,* 13 October 1980; *Sunday Times,* 19 October 1980; and *Business Week,* 20 October 1980, pp. 56–57; and 10 November 1980, p. 53.

40. See Assembly, *Debates,* 21 March 1984, cols. 3459–79.

41. "Guarding a Nation's Lifeline," *Paratus*, vol. 31, no. 3 (March 1980), p. 36.

42. "Business Security," *Management* (February 1983), pp. 75, 91.

43. See "Border Warders," *Financial Mail*, vol. 71, no. 10 (9 March 1979). *Sunday Tribune*, 21 May 1978; *Rand Daily Mail*, 3 March 1979, p. 5; 5 February 1982; and 24 May 1982, p. 2; and "Grensboere is paraat," *Paratus*, vol. 32, no. 10 (October 1981), pp. 24–27.

44. *Star*, 15 January 1983, p. 4; and 14 May 1983, p. 12.

45. *White Paper on Defence, 1984*, p. 6.

46. *White Paper on Defence, 1982*, p. 1.

47. *White Paper on Defence, 1984*, pp. 1–4.

48. Ibid., p. 2.

49. Ibid., p. 22.

50. *Financial Mail*, vol. 82, no. 3 (15 January 1982), p. 191.

51. *White Paper on Defence, 1982*, p. 28.

3. CENTRALIZATION OF STATE POWER AND THE CENTRALITY OF THE SECURITY ESTABLISHMENT

1. For a good example of a study that explicitly rejects emphasizing the role of key individuals (even though it presents a good deal of data about social background and experiences), see Ronald Weitzer, "Continuities in the Politics of State Security in Zimbabwe," in *The Political Economy of Zimbabwe*, ed. Michael Schatzberg (New York: Praeger, forthcoming). A more mechanistic institutional approach from a broadly comparative perspective is Thomas T. Mackie and Brian W. Hogwood, *Cabinet Committees in Executive Decision-Making: A Comparative Perspective* (Glasgow: Centre for the Study of Public Policy, University of Strathclyde, 1983). Studies in Public Policy No. III.

2. Hermann Giliomee, *The Parting of the Ways: South African Politics, 1976–82* (Cape Town: David Philips, 1982), p. 11. See also the discussion of executive styles in Robert I. Rotberg, "The process of Decision-Making in Contemporary South Africa," *CSIS Africa Notes*, no. 22 (28 December 1983), esp. pp. 1–2.

3. Ken Owen and Neil Hooper, *Sunday Times*, 14 October 1979; and Ivor Wilkins, *Sunday Times*, 28 September 1980, p. 31.

4. See Giliomee, "Governing in the Managerial Style," *Parting of the Ways*, pp. 34–42.

5. Brzezinski, "Deciding Who Makes Foreign Policy," *New York Times Magazine*, 18 September 1983, p. 58.

6. *South Africa: A Study in Conflict* (Berkeley: University of California Press, 1967), p. 86. Herrenvolk democracy in this context is taken to mean a democracy for whites only, in which the bonds of race lead to solidarity for all whites regardless of class, and in which class ties across racial barriers are prevented.

7. Gavin Evans, "The Role of the Military in Education in South Africa," B.A. (Hons.) dissertation, University of Cape Town, May 1983, p. 150. Frankel, in contrast, says that there is "no evidence to suggest that the Defence Force participated in the design of the new constitution through the prime minister's Constitutional Committee," although he admits that "the spirit and substance of the new pattern of constitutional arrangements meld perfectly with Defence Force conceptions of total strategy and the advancing political stakes of the military in the civilian system." *Pretoria's Praetorians*, pp. 167–68.

8. Many of these questions are posed by Deon Geldenhuys and Hennie Kotze,

"Aspects of Political Decision-Making in South Africa," *Politikon*, X, no. 1 (June 1983), pp. 42–43. A more complete discussion of the new constitution is L. J. Boulle, *Constitutional Reform and the Apartheid State: Legitimacy, Consociationalism and Control in South Africa* (New York: St. Martin's Press, 1984).

9. For more detail on these institutions see Deon Geldenhuys, *The Diplomacy of Isolation: South African Foreign Policy Making* (Johannesburg: Macmillan, 1984), pp. 141-42.

10. This account depends on a series of articles that appeared in the *Rand Daily Mail* by Mervyn Rees, 1, 2 February 1980; and also the *Star*, 14 January 1980 (daily edition), p. 2; and 23 April 1982, p. 10; *Sunday Express*, 13 December 1981; *Sunday Times*, 22 October 1978, p. 15; and Chris Vermaak, "The BOSS Man Speaks," *Scope*, 29 June 1979, pp. 16–23. Also *BOSS: The First 5 Years* (London: International Defence and Aid, 1974); and RSA, *Report of the Commission of Inquiry into Matters Relating to the Security of the State* (Abridged) [Potgieter Report] (Pretoria: Government Printer, 1971).

11. See, for example, Gordon Winter, *Inside BOSS: South Africa's Secret Police* (Harmondsworth: Penguin, 1981), pp. 557–58, 578, 580; and chap. 40, pp. 542–58.

12. *Sunday Express*, 13 December 1981.

13. *Die Transvaler* (Johannesburg), 27 August 1981; "Nuwe stelsel van Diensplig is nodig," *Paratus*, vol. 33, no. 12 (December 1982), p. 64.

14. See, for example, the *Citizen*, 29 September 1982; *Financial Mail* special supplements on "Security," vol. 89, no. 3 (15 July 1983); vol. 93, no. 7 (17 August 1984); vol. 86, no. 3 (15 October 1982), p. 294; and vol. 90, no. 9 (2 December 1983), p. 62.

15. Winter, *Inside BOSS*, pp. 320–21.

16. Evans, "Military in Education," pp. 107–11.

17. See Philip Frankel, "Pretoria's Praetorians: Civil-Military Relations in South Africa," unpublished paper, 1983, pp. 16–17; C. Wright Mills, *The Power Elite* (New York: Oxford University Press, 1956), esp. chaps. 9, 12.

18. "The business of defence," *Financial Mail*, vol. 62, no. 9 (26 November 1976), pp. 797–98; "Armscor: Behind the Secrecy Shroud," *Financial Mail*, vol. 81, no. 11 (11 September 1981), pp. 1240–41; *Sunday Times*, 11 July 1982, p. 25; RSA, DOD, *White Paper on Defence, 1982*, pp. 25–28; and *White Paper on Defence, 1984*, pp. 19–20; "Krygkor/Armscor," Supplement to *Paratus*, vol. 33, no. 11 (November 1982); *Star*, 5 September 1983, p. 8; and "Armscor Curbs Costs," *Financial Mail*, vol. 90, no. 10 (9 December 1983), p. 74. Further background and discussion of Armscor can be found in Frankel, *Pretoria's Praetorians*, pp. 81–89.

19. 1983 employment had been allowed to fall from 29,000 by not filling vacancies. Subsidiaries were urged to undertake business outside the defense sector. See *White Paper on Defence, 1984*, p. 19.

20. Lists of attenders of the Carlton and the much larger Cape of Good Hope conferences appear in Assembly, *Debates*, 15 March 1983, Q.cols. 655–77. Government accounts of the two meetings are: *Towards a Constellation of States in Southern Africa* (Pretoria: South African Information Service, 1980); and *The Good Hope Plan for Southern Africa* (Pretoria: Department of Foreign Affairs and Information, 1981).

21. Philip Frankel, "Race and Counter-Revolution: South Africa's 'Total Strategy,' " *Journal of Commonwealth and Comparative Politics*, vol. 18, no. 3 (October 1980), pp. 277–79.

22. See Geldenhuys, *Diplomacy of Isolation*, p. 143; and *White Paper on*

Defence, 1984, pp. 13–14. Frankel makes no mention of its dissolution: see *Pretoria's Praetorians*, pp. 4, 80–81.

23. The November 1977 Security Council Resolution 418, which imposed a mandatory arms embargo against South Africa. In December 1979 the U.N. General Assembly voted (124 to 7) an oil embargo.

24. *Star*, 16 April 1984, p. 8.

25. Ibid., 14 May 1983, p. 1.

26. *Guardian* (London), 27 March 1984.

27. Philip Frankel, "South Africa: The Politics of Police Control," *Comparative Politics*, vol. 12 (July 1980), pp. 481–99.

28. Kenneth W. Grundy, *Soldiers Without Politics: Blacks in the South African Armed Forces* (Berkeley: University of California Press, 1983), pp. 135–42.

29. *Plain Dealer* (Cleveland), 10 May 1983, p. 7A.

30. The publications are chiefly Geldenhuys & Kotzee, "Aspects of Political Decision-Making"; Kenneth W. Grundy, *The Rise of the South African Security Establishment: An Essay on the Changing Locus of State Power*. Bradlow Series No. 1 (Braamfontein: SAIIA, August 1983); and Simon Jenkins, "Destabilisation in Southern Africa," *Economist*, vol. 288, no. 7298 (16 July 1983), pp. 19–28.

31. Text of Lt.-Gen. van Deventer's briefing paper is printed in: "State Security Council: Not Sinister!" *Paratus*, vol 34, no. 11 (November 1983), pp. 9–11. The conference is reported in the *Star*, 26 September 1983, p. 3; *Washington Post*, 25 September 1984, pp. 1, 16; *Africa News*, XXI, no. 15 (10 October 1983), pp. 1–4, 11. Commentary on the disclosures is in *Argus* (Cape Town), 22 September 1983; *Cape Times*, 23 September 1983; and *Rapport* (Johannesburg), 25 September 1983. Lt. Gen. van Deventer became "ambassador" to Ciskei in July 1985. *Financial Mail*, vol. 96, no. 9 (31 May 1985), p. 61.

32. "Security Intelligence and State Security Act," Statutes of the Republic of South Africa, no. 64 of 1972. This provides that the prime minister must be chairman and that membership include the senior minister of the Republic, the ministers of defense, foreign affairs, justice and police, and any other ministers whom the prime minister asks to attend. In "Reaching into Government," *Financial Mail*, vol. 86, no. 2 (8 October 1982), p. 145, the SSC was reported also to include the ministers of finance, co-operation and development, internal affairs, and constitutional affairs plus a number of specified coopted senior civil servants.

33. See P.W. Botha in Assembly, *Debates*, 6 February 1980, col. 324.

34. Malan, "Die aanslag teen Suid-Afrika," in *ISSUP Strategiese Oorsig*, November 1980 as quoted in: Geldenhuys & Kotzee, "Aspects of Political Decision-Making," p. 35.

35. See P. W. Botha in Assembly, *Debates*, 26 April 1984, cols. 5241–43.

36. *Cape Times*, 23 January 1982.

37. Frankel, "Race and Counter-Revolution," p. 277.

38. See the portrait of Barnard in: *Financial Mail*, vol. 84, no. 10 (4 June 1982), p. 1131.

39. Evans, "Military in Education," p. 32.

4. THE MILITARIZATION OF WHITE SOCIETY

1. The term "war psychosis" is from Evans, "Military in Education," p. 3. "Psychosis of peace" is attributed to G. P. D. Terblanch, Assembly, *Debates*, 17 May 1984, col. 6801.

2. The most complete study of this subject is found in Evans, ibid. See also Frankel, *Pretoria's Praetorians*, pp. 98–100.

3. See, for example, "Kadette hul skool se trots," *Paratus*, vol. 34, no. 8

(August 1983), pp. 76–77. Data on cadet detachments is published in Assembly, *Debates*, 24 May 1984, *Q*.col. 1333.

4. A list of Coloured and Indian schools visited appears in Assembly, *Debates*, 17 August 1983, *Q*.cols. 1866–69.

5. See, for example, the *Citizen*, 20 July 1982, p. 14; and "Spotlight on our Youth: Veld and Vlei course good for National Service," *Paratus*, vol. 34, no. 4 (April 1983), pp. 20–21.

6. See *Rand Daily Mail*, 3 June 1982, pp. 1, 6; *Star*, 3 June 1982 (daily edition), p. 11; *Sunday Express*, 13 June 1982, p. 13; and *Paratus*, vol. 35, no. 3 (March 1984), pp. 24–25.

7. Evans, "Military in Education," pp.66–67.

8. *Star*, 29 September 1983, p. 8.

9. Terence Moll, "The Steel Crocodile: An Analysis of the Role of the Military Establishment in the South African Social Formation, with Particular Reference to *Paratus*," Southern African Economic History: Long Essay, 9 October 1981, University of Cape Town, pp. 20–22.

10. Assembly, *Debates*, 7 September 1983, *Q*.cols. 2069–76. See also Frankel, *Pretoria's Praetorians*, pp. 97–98.

11. See, for example, the editorial in *Die Transvaler*, 9 February 1984, in which it was argued that if the SADF wishes to keep the nation behind it, it will have to consider disclosing more in the future than it did in the past. English translation in *South Africa Digest*, 17 February 1984, pp. 22–23.

12. "Winners, Losers, Bummers," *Plain Dealer*, 22 December 1983.

13. See *Sunday Express*, 30 March 1980, pp. 1–2.

14. SADF thinking on this matter is exemplified by Maj. Gen. C.J. Lloyd, "The Importance of Rural Development in the Defence Strategy of South Africa and the need for Private Sector Involvement," Seminar delivered to the Urban Foundation, Natal Region, Durban, 10 August 1979. The WHAM campaigns are described in detail in Evans, "Military in Education," pp. 155–202.

15. *Post* (Johannesburg), 31 January 1980; and *Sunday Post* (Johannesburg), 2 September 1979.

16. *Sunday Post*, 10 February 1980.

17. For example, *Rand Daily Mail*, 13 June 1979.

18. Assembly, *Debates*, 17 April 1978, cols. 4919–23, among others.

19. Ibid., 25 March 1980, cols. 3502–15 (prime minister); and cols. 3477–82 (Dr. Slabbert).

20. *Voice*, vol. 4, no. 13 (April 1980), p. 2. See also student criticism of Dr. Slabbert's naivité in the pamphlet *Army News* (Johannesburg: Milcom, Student Representative Council, Witwatersrand University, 1980), p. 2.

21. On this episode, see *Sunday Times*, 23 March 1980, p. 1; and 30 March 1980, p. 20; *Rand Daily Mail*, 24 March 1980, pp. 1–2; 25 March 1980, p. 12; 26 March 1980, pp. 1–2, 4; and 31 March 1980, p. 7; *Sunday Express*, 30 March 1980, pp. 1–2, 8–9; and Assembly, *Debates*, 24 March 1980, col. 3325; and 25 March 1980, cols. 3477–515.

22. Assembly, *Debates*, 2 February 1984, cols. 338–40; 24 February 1984, *Q*.cols. 336–41; and 7 March 1984, *Q*.cols. 516–25.

23. *Sunday Express*, 4 September 1983.

24. Assembly, *Debates*, 8 June 1983, *Q*.col. 1487.

25. Philip Myburgh (PFP) in ibid., 21 March 1983, cols. 3551–59.

26. For comparative materials, see Morris Janowitz and Stephen D. Wesbrook,

eds., *The Political Education of Soldiers*, Sage Research Series on War, Revolution, and Peacekeeping, vol. 11 (Beverly Hills, Calif.: Sage, 1983).

27. Assembly, *Debates*, 22 April 1975, cols. 4569–74; and *Rand Daily Mail*, 25 April 1975, p. 2.

28. *Rand Daily Mail*, 22 March 1984.

29. Assembly, *Debates*, 17 August 1983, Q.cols. 1895–97.

30. Ibid., 19 May 1982, Q.col. 861.

31. Ibid., 6 May 1975, Q.cols. 886–87.

32. *Cape Times*, 6 August 1982, p. 3.

33. See, for example, J.S. Pansegrow (NP) in Assembly, *Debates*, 13 June 1975, cols. 9307–08.

34. *White Paper on Defence, 1984*, p. 20.

35. "South Africa: Countering the Threat of Sanctions," *Business Week*, 20 November 1978; and "South Africa Driving a Perilous Road to Diesel Self-Reliance," *Business Week*, 16 June 1980. Data on the early operation of the Atlantis diesel facility can be found in Assembly, *Debates*, 17 March 1983, Q.cols. 706–08: and 22 February 1984, Q.col. 286. More positive data is in *Financial Mail*, vol. 91, no. 7 (17 February 1984), pp. 90–92.

36. *White Paper on Defence, 1984*, p. 20.

37. See Kenneth W. Grundy, "On Domesticating Transnational Corporations: South Africa and the Automotive Industry," *Journal of Commonwealth and Comparative Politics*, vol. 19, no. 2 (July 1981), pp. 157–73.

38. *Star*, 13 September 1976 (daily edition); Assembly, *Debates*, 20 May 1983, col. 7561.

39. *White Paper on Defence, 1984*, p. 16.

40. Ibid., pp. 12–13.

41. Frankel calls the Commando "a powerful social metaphor," in *Pretoria's Praetorians*, pp. 19–28.

5. A STRATEGIC CONSTELLATION OF STATES AND POLICY TOWARD THE HOMELANDS

1. See Kenneth W. Grundy, "South Africa's Regional Defense Plans: The Homeland Armies," in *South Africa in Southern Africa: The Intensifying Vortex of Violence*, ed. Thomas M. Callaghy (New York: Praeger, 1983), pp. 133–51.

2. See Deon Geldenhuys, *South Africa's Black Homelands: Past Objectives, Present Realities and Future Developments* (Johannesburg: SAIIA, 1981), pp. 40–41.

3. The literature on homeland dependence is extensive. For a survey of some of the earlier materials see Kenneth W. Grundy, "A Review of Scholarly Literature on Pretoria's Homelands Scheme," *Journal of Southern African Affairs*, III, no. 2 (April 1978), pp. 225–34. Other important studies include: Jeffrey Butler, Robert I. Rotberg, and John Adams, *The Black Homelands of South Africa: The Political and Economic Development of Bophuthatswana and KwaZulu* (Berkeley: University of California Press, 1977); Barry Streek and Richard Wicksteed, *Render Unto Kaiser: A Transkei Dossier* (Johannesburg: Ravan Press, 1981); and Roger Southall, *South Africa's Transkei: The Political Economy of an "Independent" Bantustan* (New York; Monthly Review Press, 1983).

4. Assembly, *Debates*, 5 April 1978, col. 3955.

5. Ibid., 6 March 1963, col. 2265.

6. Ibid., 7 March 1963, col. 2356.

7. Ibid., 26 January 1963, col. 271.

8. Ibid., 20 May 1959, col. 6227; 29 March 1962, col. 3458.

9. See "Border Conflict: 'The Grass is Greener . . .'," *Indicator South Africa: Rural Monitor*, I, no. 3 (1983), pp. 3–5.

10. See *Africa News*, XXI, no. 7 (15 August 1983), p. 8; *Star*, 20 February 1984, p. 12; *New York Times*, 24 July 1983; *Financial Mail*, vol. 89, no. 5 (29 July 1983), pp. 61, 63; or South African Institute of Race Relations [hereinafter cited as SAIRR], *Survey of Race Relations in South Africa, 1982* (Johannesburg: SAIRR 1983), pp. 387–89.

11. See, for example, Streek & Wicksteed, *Render Unto Kaiser*; and *'Homeland' Tragedy: Function and Force*. DSG/SARS Information Publication 6. (Johannesburg: Southern African Research Service and Development Studies Group, August 1982).

12. *Africa News*, XXI, no. 21 (21 November 1983), pp. 6–8; Humphrey Berkeley, "The Mission that Failed," *The Spectator*, no. 243 (4 August 1979), pp. 12–14.

13. See Grundy, *Soldiers without Politics*, pp. 231–41.

14. P. W. Botha in Assembly, *Debates*, 22 April 1975, col. 4584.

15. Quoted in *Rand Daily Mail*, 27 May 1980.

16. Ibid., 3 August 1974.

17. *Financial Mail*, vol. 89, no. 12 (16 September 1983), p. 46–47.

18. See Patrick Laurence, *The Transkei: South Africa's Politics of Partition* (Johannesburg: Ravan Press, 1976), p. 131.

19. See SAIRR, *Survey of Race Relations in South Africa, 1980* (Johannesburg: SAIRR, 1981), p. 422.

20. This idea is borrowed, with some considerable alteration, from Francis Wilson, "Towards Economic Justice in South Africa," a paper prepared for the 50th anniversary conference of the South African Institute of Race Relations, Johannesburg, 4 July 1979, particularly pp. 23–30. Prof. Wilson is applying a similar model to the issue of labor linkages between the RSA and its neighbors.

21. *South Africa Digest*, 6 April 1984, p. 3.

22. See Alan R. Booth, *Swaziland: Tradition and Change in a Southern African Kingdom* (Boulder, Colo.: Westview Press, 1983), pp. 118–20; and Philip Bonner, *Kings, Commoners and Concessionaires: The Evolution and Dissolution of the Nineteenth-century Swazi State* (Cambridge: Cambridge University Press, 1983).

23. *Star*, 23 April 1984, p. 1.

24. *Washington Post*, 21 June 1984.

25. The agreement with Transkei is in Republic of South Africa, *Government Gazette*, vol. 136, no. 5320 (22 october 1976), p. 26; with Bophuthatswana in *Government Gazette*, vol. 150, no. 5923 (6 December 1977), pp. 34–34; and with Venda it is reprinted in *'Homeland' Tragedy*, p. 21. The agreement with Ciskei is in *Government Gazette*, vol. 203, no. 8294 (14 May 1982), pp. 1–7.

26. See Gail-Maryse Cockram, *South West African Mandate* (Cape Town: Juta, 1976), p. 40.

27. One South African journalist, Brendan Nicholson, has already referred to the emerging security system in the region as a "Warsaw Pact-style buffer of states." *Star*, 23 April 1984, p. 10.

28. See the arguments advanced in C.E.J. Stephan and H. Booysen, "The Angolan Conflict: Its Relevance for South Africa in her Relations with Future Independent Bantustans and the Need for a Monroe Doctrine," *South African*

Yearbook of International Law, 1975, vol. 1 (Pretoria: University of South Africa, 1976), pp. 103–14.

29. See Deon Geldenhuys, *South Africa's Black Homelands,* pp. 51–78, for a discussion of the alternatives.

30. *Address by the Hon. P.W. Botha, MP, Prime Minister, Minister of Defence and of the National Intelligence Service at the Opening of the Summit Meeting in Pretoria on* 23 July 1980 (Pretoria: Department of Foreign Affairs and Information, *1980*), p. 7.

31. See, for example, P.W. Botha's speech at the signing of the Nkomati accord, in *Paratus,* vol. 35, no. 4 (April 1984), pp. 6–7, 14.

32. See the Defence appropriation debate for 1984: Assembly, *Debates,* 17 May 1984, cols. 6795, 6800; and 18 May 1984, col. 6927; and the laudatory tone regarding the SADF throughout, cols. 6738–6932.

6. FOREIGN POLICY

1. *White Paper on Defence, 1984,* p. 3. This view is expressed in practically the same words, by National Party spokesmen. See Assembly, *Debates,* 17 May 1984, cols. 6799–6802.

2. An early and somewhat speculative account is Robin Hallett, "The South African Intervention in Angola, 1975–76," *African Affairs,* vol. 77, no. 308 (July 1978), pp. 347–86. More recent data is included in Geldenhuys, *The Diplomacy of Isolation,* pp. 75–84.

3. See Chris Vermaak, "The BOSS Man Speaks," *Scope,* 29 June 1979, pp. 16–23, esp. pp. 21–22.

4. Geldenhuys, *The Diplomacy of Isolation,* p. 79.

5. Ibid.

6. *Times* (London), 30 December 1975.

7. Hallett, "South African Intervention," p. 370; quoting Robert Moss of the *Sunday Telegraph* (London). Geldenhuys seems to place greater emphasis on P.W. Botha's special role in the Angolan war, but he also argues that Defence was upset by the lack of a clear political line to follow. The very mudiness of South African policy on Angola is testimony that P.W. Botha alone did not have his way. The doves were able to confuse policy, and to them, that represented a "victory" of sorts, given Defence's advantages. *The Diplomacy of Isolation,* pp. 82–83.

8. See the *Guardian* (London), 8 August 1979, p. 6.

9. See Willem Steenkamp, *Borderstrike!: South Africa into Angola* (Durban: Butterworth, 1983). See also Geldenhuys, *The Diplomacy of Isolation,* p. 83.

10. *Citizen,* 27 December 1982; *Rand Daily Mail,* 27 December 1982; and *International Herald Tribune,* 27 December 1982.

11. *Star,* 28 January 1985, p. 8.

12. Simon Jenkins, "Destabilisation in Southern Africa," *Economist,* vol. 288, no. 7298 (16 July 1983), pp. 19–28.

13. South African responses to accusations of destabilization are: Ashley C. Lillie, "Destabilisation in Southern Africa Perspective," *Paratus,* vol. 34, no. 3 (March 1983), pp. 48–51; no. 4 (April 1983), pp. 30–31, 65; and R.K. Campbell, "Support for Cross-border Strikes," *Paratus,* vol. 34, no. 4 (April 1983), pp. 10–11.

14. On SADF destruction of civilian targets see the *Guardian,* 29 January and 2 February 1981.

15. See the series by Jay Ross in *Washington Post*, 6 April and 8 April 1983.

16. See the *Star*, 23 April 1984, pp. 10, 12; and 15 October 1984, p. 15; "Nkomati under Strain," *Financial Mail*, vol. 94, no. 9 (30 November 1984), p. 45; "Saving Nkomati," *Financial Mail*, vol. 95, no. 3 (18 January 1985), p. 45; "Nkomati Egg-dance," *Financial Mail*, vol. 95, no. 4 (25 January 1985), p. 47; and Herbert M. Howe, "Mozambique: Military Weakness Led to Cease-fire with S. Africa," *Christian Science Monitor*, 18 October 1984.

17. *Star*, 22 August 1983, p. 7.

18. Ibid., 2 April 1983, p. 3; 15 August 1983, p. 4; *Washington Post*, 13 April 1984; and *Times*, 23 April 1984.

19. See Jonathan Steele, "Pretoria's secret war against Zimbabwe," *Guardian*, 30 April 1984.

20. Lillie, "Destabilisation in Southern Africa," part 1, p. 49.

21. Assembly, *Debates*, 13 February 1984, Q.cols. 148–49.

22. See *Star*, 16 June 1982 (daily edition), pp. 1, 3.

23. Assembly, *Debates*, 13 February 1984, Q.cols. 148–49.

24. See Peter Vale, "South Africa as a Pariah International State," paper presented to a symposium sponsored by the South African Institute of Race Relations and the South African Institute of International Affairs, 12 November 1977.

25. "No place to hide for terrorists," *Paratus*, vol. 34, no. 11 (November 1983), p. 17.

26. See Derek W. Bowett, "The Interrelation of Theories of Intervention and Self-Defense," in *Law and Civil War in the Modern World*, ed. John Norton Moore (Baltimore: Johns Hopkins University Press, 1974), pp. 38–50.

27. *White Paper on Defence, 1984*, p. 28.

28. Chester A. Crocker, *South Africa's Defense Posture: Coping and Vulnerability*, The Washington Papers, vol. 9, no. 84 (Beverly Hills & London: Sage Publications, 1981), p. 85.

29. John de St. Jorre, "Pax Pretoriana," *New Republic*, no. 3611 (2 April 1984), pp. 20–23. The links between force and diplomacy are also pointed up in "The message from Cuvelai," *Financial Mail*, vol. 91, no. 2 (13 January 1984), pp. 30–31; and in Robert M. Price, "Pretoria's Southern African Strategy," *African Affairs*, vol. 83, no. 330 (January 1984), pp. 11–32; and Klaus Freiherr von der Ropp, "Southern Africa Under the Sign of the Pax Pretoriana," *Aussenpolitik*, no. 4 (1984), pp. 415–29.

30. As quoted in *New York Times*, 11 october 1983.

31. As quoted in *Financial Mail*, vol. 92, no. 1 (6 April 1984), pp. 48–49.

32. Brink is a popular Afrikaner novelist, highly critical of his peoples' inhumane treatment of their fellow South Africans. See his *Rumours of Rain* (London: W.H. Allen, 1978).

33. For the impact of the Nkomati Accord and the Swaziland-South African nonaggression pact on the ANC, see *Washington Post*, 16 April 1984.

7. CONCLUSIONS

1. *New York Times*, 2 November 1983, p. 10.

2. Gore Vidal, *The Second American Revolution and Other Essays (1976–1982)* (New York: Random House, 1982), p. 152.

3. Caryle Murphy in *International Herald Tribune*, 31 May, 1 June 1980, p. 3.

4. This was disclosed by Dr. Seiler in testimony before the United States House of Representatives Subcommittees on International Economic Policy and

Trade in Africa and on International Organizations; U.S. Congress, House of Representatives, Committee on Foreign Affairs, *U.S. Policy Toward South Africa*, 96th Congress, 2nd session, 1980, p. 46. Dr. Seiler later said that this information had been confirmed by at least three different people; *Star*, 7 May 1980 (daily edition), p. 1.

5. William H. McNeill, *The Pursuit of Power* (Chicago: University of Chicago Press, 1982), pp. 9–23.

6. *Constitution of the United States of America*: Article I, Section VIII, Clauses 11, 12, 14, 15 & 17; Section X, Clause 3; Article II, Section II, Clause 1; and Amendments II and III.

7. See, for example, *Financial Mail*, vol. 77, no. 10 (5 September 1980), pp. 1084–85.

8. Harry Schwarz as quoted in *Financial Mail*, vol. 86, no. 2 (8 October 1982), p. 144.

9. *Plain Dealer* (Cleveland), 22 December 1983, p. 4A.

INDEX

Items marked with an asterisk are explained more fully in the Glossary.

Academics in security establishment, 44–45
African National Congress, * 12, 28, 32, 42, 61, 66, 80, 82, 101, 103, 105, 106
  in Botswana, 100
  in Lesotho, 97–98, 99
  in Mozambique, 95–97
  in Swaziland, 100
  in Zimbabwe, 99
Afrikaner power structure, 3–5, 8–9
Afrikanervolkswag, 5, 65
Algeria, 27
Angola, 2, 9, 20, 31–32, 53, 83, 88–92, 95, 105
"Area Defence," 28–29
Armed forces. See SADF
Armscor, * 6, 45–48, 122n
Atomic Energy Act, amended 1979, 46–47, 69

Barlow Rand, 46
Barnard, Dr. Lukas Daniel, 44
Basuto Democratic Alliance, 98
Basutoland Congress Party, * 98
Basutoland National Party, * 98
Bell, Fred, 48
Bophuthatswana, 71, 72–73, 78–79, 83
Border defense, 30–31
Botha, R. F. "Pik," 1, 80, 86, 87, 96, 97, 98, 106, 110–11
Botswana, 100
Brezhnev doctrine, 76–77, 84
Brink, Andre, 106
Broder, David S., 60
Broederbond, 4–5
Brzezinski, Zbigniew, 38
Budgets, defense, 19–21, 119n
Bureau for State Security (BOSS), * 38, 42–44, 45, 56, 89, 91, 92
Business community, 4–5, 46–48, 85, 119n, 122n
Buthelezi, Chief Gatsha, 66, 79

Cabinet committee system, 51–55
Cadet detachments, 59
Cahora Bassa, 86, 102

Cape Housing Action Committee, 66
Central Intelligence Organization (Rhodesia), * 91
Ciskei, 71, 73, 75, 77, 79, 83, 97
Civic Action, 28, 60–62
"Civic guidance," 65–66
Coetsee, H.J. "Kobie," 44, 75
Communist Party of South Africa, 42
Comores Islands, 97
Confederation, regional, 85–87
Conservative Party, * 3–4, 6, 16, 25, 40, 64–65, 67
Constellation of Southern African States, * 13, 85–87
Constitution of 1983, 39–41, 65, 67, 121n
Cooperation and Development, Department of, 80, 81, 82
Council for Scientific and Industrial Research, * 21, 45, 46
Crocker, Chester, 105–106
Cross-border strikes, 88–106
Cuba, 90–91, 92, 103
Customs Union, 97–98, 102
Czechoslovakia, 84

de St. Jorre, John, 106
Defence Act of 1957, 22, 27
Defence Advisory Council, 47
Defence Amendment Act of 1982, 29
Defence Manpower Liaison Committee, * 41, 47
Defence Research and Development Council, 47
Density of Population in Designated Areas Act of 1979, 31
Destabilization, 2, 88–92, 94–106
  See also Preemptive Intervention
DFA or DFAI. See Foreign Affairs, Department of
Diesel industry, 68
Disinformation, by armed forces, 66
Dolinchek, Martin, 101
Domestic unrest, 26–31, 112–13
  use of armed force against, 7
DONS. See National Security, Department of
Dulles, John Foster, 14
du Plessis, Barend, 50

du Plessis, Dr. J.E., 55
Dutch Reformed Church, 4–5
Dutton, Lt. Gen. Jack, 108

Economic self-sufficiency, 67–70
Education, 58–59, 61, 65
English-speakers, in SADF, 8–9
Executive State, rise of, 38–39

Foreign Affairs, Department of, * 38, 50, 53, 55, 56, 81, 83, 85, 87, 107–108
Fourie, Brand, 2, 89
France, 14
Frankel, Philip, 45

GBS. * See Joint Management Centres
Geldenhuys, Deon, 48, 89–90
Geldenhuys, Lt. Gen. Jannie, 93
General Motors (SA), 68
Germany, 84, 97
Gqabi, Joe, 99
Graaff, Sir de Villiers, 72
Great Britain, 14, 97

Hartzenberg, Dr. Ferdie, 25
Herstigte Nasionale Party, * 3–4, 6, 25, 67
Homelands, 26, 77–82
  consolidation of, 56, 77–82
  defense of, 71–75, 85
Horwood, Dr. Owen, 110–11
Hot pursuit, doctrine of, 103
Human Sciences Research Council, * 45, 56, 60

Immigrants, military obligation, 23
Information, Department of, 38, 43, 45, 92
Information scandal, 35, 43
Ingwavuma land deal, 66, 76, 79–82
Inkatha, 66
Institute for Marine Technology, 21
Institute for Strategic Studies, 44–45
Intelligence services, 6, 9, 21, 32, 38, 42–44, 73. *See also* Bureau for State Security; Military Intelligence Section; National Intelligence Service; National Security, Department of; Republican Intelligence; Security Police
Iscor, * 46
Israel, 20

Joint Defence College, 41–42, 119n

Joint Management Centres, * 52–53
Jooste, G.P., 2

KaNgwane. *See* Ingwavumua land deal
Kapstein, Jonathan, 27
KEOSSA, * 56
Korea, South, 20
Koornhof, Dr. Piet, 80, 82
KwaZulu, 66, 76, 79, 82

Labour Party (Coloured), 25
Lebanon, 112
Lesotho, 2, 79, 81, 95, 97–99
Lesotho Liberation Army, * 95, 98–99
Lloyd, Maj. Gen. Charles, 93
Lodge, Tom, 12

McGiven, Arthur, 43
McNeill, William H., 109
Malan, Gen. Magnus, 18, 36, 41, 47, 56, 59, 63, 64, 101–102, 108, 110–12
  on Angola, 53
  economic strength, 69
  political strategy, 27–28, 62
  on State Security Council, 53
  on "total onslaught," 11
Malawi, 97
Malaysia, 27
Malenkov, Georgi, 54
Managerial revolution, 34–36
Mandela, Nelson, 61
Mangope, Lucas, 72–73
Manpower Utilization, Department of, 47
Maree, John, 46
Marxism, 11–13, 15–16, 47
Military Academy (Saldanha Bay), 41, 108, 119n
Military industrial complex, 45–48
Military Intelligence Section, * 6, 42–44, 60, 66, 89, 91, 100
Mills, C. Wright, 45, 48
Minnaar, Taillefer, 73
MNR. * See Renamo
Mokhehle, Ntsu, 98
Monroe doctrine, 76–77, 83
Morris, Michael, 45
Mozambique, 2, 9, 26, 79, 91, 95–97, 105
Mugabe, Robert, 91, 99
Mulder, Connie, 89
Muller, Hilgard, 2, 88–89
Munger, Edwin, 2
Muzorewa, Bishop Abel, 86, 99

Namibia, 9, 12, 24, 26, 31, 54, 61, 62, 66, 86, 89, 92–94, 95
National Intelligence Service, * 6, 21, 30, 38, 42–44, 51, 53, 56, 100–101
National Key Points Act of 1980, 30, 45, 69
National Party, * 3–5, 6, 8, 16–18, 32, 36, 38, 40, 63–65, 78, 92, 110–12
National Security, Department of (DONS), * 38, 44, 56
National Supplies Procurement Act of 1970, 46–47, 69
New Republic Party, * 6, 27, 63
Nkomati accord, 83, 86, 91
Nonaggression, treaties of, 81–82, 83–85
Ntoula, Revelation, 64

Orderly Movement and Settlement of Black Persons Bill, 56

Pan Africanist Congress *, 42
Paratus, 17
Partisan politics, SADF involvement in, 62–67
People's army, concept of, 110
Petroleum Products Amendment Act of 1979, 46–47, 69
Physical planning, 69, 81
Professionalization of SADF, 69–70
Pirow, Oswald, 8
Police, 6, 8, 9, 28, 48, 50, 53, 56, 72, 91
    budgets, 19–21
    COIN units, 24, 62
    force levels, 19–21
    See also Security Police
Political component of strategy, 27–28
Poqo, * 42
Portugal, 97, 102
Preemptive intervention, doctrine of, 2, 84–85, 102–106
Press, 4, 56, 59–60
Pretoria, University of, 44–45
Pretorius, Maj. Gen. Phil, 61, 63–64
Progressive Federal Party, * 6, 12, 25, 27, 40, 62, 63–65, 67
Psychological Action Plan (of SADF), 63–64, 66
Public opinion polls, 12
Public Service Commission, 52
Publications Control Board, 59

QwaQwa, 79, 98

"Radio Truth," 99
Rationalization of government, 34–36
Raw, W. Vause, 27
Reagan, Ronald, 14–15
Reid-Daly, Col. Ron, 45
Renamo, * 91, 95–97
Republican Intelligence, 42, 45
Resistência Nacional Moçambicana. *See* Renamo
Rhoodie, Dr. Eschel, 91
Roos, Brig. Ben, 27
Roux, Dr. J.P., 50
Rural defense, 30–31

SABC, * 60
SADF, * 6, 17
    black members, 23–25, 75–76
    budgets, 19–21, 119n
    Cadets, 58–59
    Civic Action, 28, 60–62
    composition, 21–25, 31, 75–76
    force levels, 19–23, 119n
    involvement in politics, 7–10, 62–67, 108–11
    leadership, 36–37, 41, 93, 108–109
    National Service, 21–22
    press relations, 59–60
    relations with academics, 44–45
    role in policy making, 1–3, 35–37, 40, 47, 49–57, 67–70, 92–94, 107–13
    SAP, 48, 72
    Strategic Planning Section, 9–10
    strategic thinking, 10–18, 26–33, 56–57, 73–77, 88–90, 94–95, 102–106, 109
    See also numerous other items in Index
Safmarine, * 48
SAP. * *See* Police
Sasol, * 46, 68
S.A. Transport Services, 51
Schwarz, Harry, 27
Sebe, Charles, 73
Sebe, Lennox, 73
Security Police, 6, 42–44, 100
Security establishment, 2, 5–6, 112–13
    defined, 41
    components of, 41–48
Seiler, John, 108
Seychelles, attempted coup, 100–101
Shangaan Battalion, 76
Slabbert, Dr. Frederick Van Zyl, 63–64
Smith, Ian D., 91, 99

Smuts, Gen. Jan Christian, 7, 8, 84
Sobuza II, King, 79–80, 82
Sole, Donald, 2
Southern African Development Coordination Conference, 81, 86–87
Soviet Union, 11–18, 31–32, 49, 50, 54, 78, 88, 97, 101
Soweto, * 61
Stalin, Joseph, 14
State Security Council, * 6, 9, 38, 40–42, 43, 49–55, 56, 68, 81, 86, 92–94, 111–12, 123n
Stellenbosch, University of, 41
Steyn Commission of Inquiry into the Mass Media, 56, 60
Strategic thinking, 9–18
Sutton-Pryce, Edward, 99
SWAPO, * 24, 26, 29, 32, 92–94, 95, 103, 105
Swart, Ray, 62
SWATF, * 24, 62, 93
Swazi Battalion, 76
Swaziland, 66, 76, 79–82, 95, 96, 100
Switzerland, 20

Tanzania, 97
Terrorism Research Centre, * 45
Thebehali, David, 61
Tires, radial, 68
Total National Strategy, 18, 49, 71, 85, 102
"Total onslaught," 1, 10–18, 49, 55, 71, 107
Transkei, 61, 71, 73, 75, 77, 78–79, 97–98
Transkeian Defence Force, 61, 73, 75, 98
Trinquier, Roger, 27
Tutu, Bishop Desmond, 12

Umkonto we Sizwe, 42
Union Defence Force, * 7–9

UNISA, * 45
UNITA, * 90, 95, 103
United Party, * 72, 73
United States, 14–15, 20, 38, 112
Universities, 4

van den Bergh, Gen. Hendrik, 42–43, 88, 91
van den Berghe, Pierre, 38
van der Merwe, Koos, 67
van der Walt Commission, 56, 77
van der Westhuizen, Gen. P.W., 93, 120n
van Deventer, Gen. A. J., 50, 53, 55, 93
Venda, 71, 73, 76, 79, 83
Verwoerd, Dr. H.F., 2, 5, 35, 72
Vidal, Gore, 107
Viljoen, Gen. Constand, 26, 28–29, 32, 41, 77, 94, 99–100, 108
Viljoen, Dr. Gerrit, 110–11
Voice of Free Africa, 96
Vorster, J.B., 3, 5, 17–18, 34–35, 42–43, 49, 51, 54, 83, 88–89, 91, 92

Walvis Bay, 54
Warsaw Pact, 84, 126n
Webster, Maj. Gen. Neil, 120n
Wilking, Louis, 68
"Winning Hearts and Minds," * 56, 60–62, 109
Winter, Gordon, 43, 45
World War I, 7
World War II, 7–8

Zambia, 104, 105
Zimbabwe, 2, 9, 48, 77, 79, 81, 86, 91, 95, 99–100, 103, 104
Zulu Battalion, 75, 76

SOCIAL SCIENCE LIBRARY

Oxford University Library Services
Manor Road
Oxford OX1 3UQ
Tel: (2)71093 (enquiries and renewals)
http://www.ssl.ox.ac.uk

This is a NORMAL LOAN item.

We will email you a reminder before this item is due.

Please see http://www.ssl.ox.ac.uk/lending.html
for details on:

- loan policies; these are also displayed on the
  notice boards and in our library guide.

- how to check when your books are due back.

- how to renew your books, including information
  on the maximum number of renewals.
  Items may be renewed if not reserved by
  another reader. Items must be renewed before
  the library closes on the due date.

- level of fines; fines are charged on overdue books.

Please note that this item may be recalled during Term.